808·51

D1460106

Speak
Easy

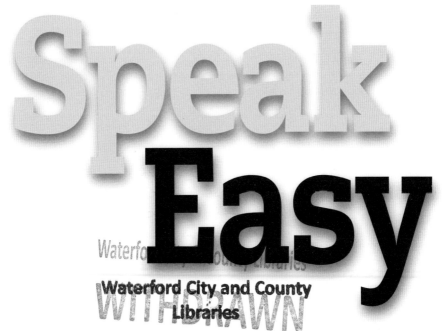

Speak Easy

THE ESSENTIAL GUIDE TO
SPEAKING IN PUBLIC

MAGGIE EYRE

Waterford City and County Libraries

WITHDRAWN

EXISLE
PUBLISHING

This edition published 2016
First published 2003 and revised in 2007

Exisle Publishing Pty Ltd
'Moonrising', Narone Creek Road, Wollombi, NSW 2325, Australia
P.O. Box 60–490, Titirangi, Auckland 0642, New Zealand
www.exislepublishing.com

Copyright © 2003, 2007 and 2016 in text: Maggie Eyre

Maggie Eyre asserts the moral right to be identified as the author
of this work.

All rights reserved. Except for short extracts for the purpose of
review, no part of this book may be reproduced, stored in a retrieval
system or transmitted in any form or by any means, whether
electronic, mechanical, photocopying, recording or otherwise,
without prior written permission from the publisher.

A CiP record for this book is available from the National Library
of Australia

ISBN 978 1 921966 85 9

Design and typesetting by Big Cat Design
Illustrations by Jane Eyre
Typeset in Sabon 10.75 on 15.45pt
Printed in China

This book uses paper sourced under ISO 14001 guidelines from
well-managed forests and other controlled sources.

10 9 8 7 6 5 4 3 2 1

Disclaimer
While this book is intended as a general information resource and
all care has been taken in compiling the contents, this book does not
take account of individual circumstances. Neither the author nor the
publisher and their distributors can be held responsible for any loss,
claim or action that may arise from reliance on the information
contained in this book.

Maggie Eyre is the Director of Fresh Eyre, a niche training company specializing in teaching presentation and media skills. Her team of journalists, voice coaches, actors and camera operators provides programmes to help transform hesitant speakers into confident communicators. Maggie has over 30 years' experience in business, public relations, education and theatre. Her work has been recognized in *Time* magazine and in international media from the UK to Dubai. She is guided by the principles of equality, integrity and compassion, with her motto being 'Never give up on anyone.' To learn more about Maggie, please visit: www.maggieeyre.com

'This programme has changed my life — this is the greatest compliment I can give you. Thank you.'
— *Sally Heyes, former Manager, Price Waterhouse Coopers Worldwide*

'The Supplier Competition was the single most important event to shape the future of Jarvis. Success would guarantee survival and set the foundation to grow and develop the business. Maggie made a huge impact, not only in helping us prepare for a presentation that won the £65 million of business, but also in getting us to challenge the way we do things and live our value.'
— *Mike Houghtan, Former Fast Line Managing Director, Network Rail, Great Britain*

'Exhausting — but extremely valuable! Much more than a presentation skills course — more an overall self-belief and esteem programme.'
— *Ant Davison, Westpac Institutional Bank, London*

'Maggie has trained over 100 of our local staff, from management trainees to board members. She worked with me to coach the winning design team for a NZD1.2 billion hydro-electric project. This was a most demanding pitch involving 17 people from five organizations.'
— *Simon Walter, Former General Manager of Marketing, Beca Carter Hollings & Ferner Ltd (New Zealand)*

'On several occasions we have utilized the services of Maggie Eyre for the training and development of senior management team members in presentation skills and to help them strengthen their professional presence. We have found Maggie exceptionally talented in developing confidence and improving the performance of the staff. I am pleased to recommend her for any similar training requirements.'
— *Rick Mayes, former Operations Director, Parsons Brinckerhoff, Dubai*

'In the world of executive search, we are regularly exposed to the broad continuum of capabilities. Every so often someone stands out with a totally unique offering — Maggie Eyre is one such person. Maggie stands out from her peer group because of her special personal qualities. She is intelligent, quick minded, practical and highly motivated. Maggie's uniqueness comes from her ability to build a rapport with her audience, put them at ease, and then take them through a graduated process of confidence building in an area where they typically have very little confidence — the domain of training and public speaking.'
— *Gary Dick, Principal at Gary Dick Advisory*

'Maggie is one of life's great enthusiasts, a huge advantage in the world of professional communications. She's also very warm, empathetic and supportive to her clients. With her theatrical training, public relations experience and natural stage presence, these qualities combine to make her a highly effective performance coach. Maggie is equally at home preparing clients to face the media or a live audience.'
— *Peter Coe, Executive Director at Tudor Reilly Health, London*

'If you want a unique style and fresh approach then look no further.'
Sarah Williams, Senior Account Director, Porter Novelli

'I was somewhat anxious about speaking in public, and watching others, was never satisfied with my own performance. Maggie's sessions have given me a notable boost in confidence; the confidence to be myself and to build my own style. The failsafe formula she prescribes in preparing for such occasions has enhanced my ability to remain confident and calm at all my speaking engagements. In my latest role I also engaged Maggie to work with some of our team in New York. They were equally as enthusiastic about the way that Maggie was able to help them overcome fears, and realize their own attributes to play on their natural strengths.'
— *Jane Cunliffe, former New Zealand Consul General and Investment Director North America, New Zealand Trade and Enterprise*

Contents

Foreword

These days, having the confidence and skills to deliver clear public messages, to present well, and to engage an audience, are seen as a requirement for success in many kinds of jobs.

Those of us who have made hundreds and even thousands of speeches over the years may often believe our significant experience has taught us how to deliver speeches effectively. But that is not always the case. Thus many seek advice on public speaking from those like Maggie Eyre who specialize in presentation skills.

I first consulted Maggie after I became Leader of the Opposition in New Zealand. She helped me to improve my overall presentation to my long-term benefit, and through my subsequent time as Prime Minister. Her tips and techniques continue to stand me in good stead in my current role at the United Nations.

I am delighted that Maggie's book *Speak Easy* continues to go from strength to strength and that this new edition will find an even wider global audience, allowing many more to benefit from her expert advice.

Helen Clark

Helen Clark
Administrator of the United Nations Development Programme

Introduction

You were not born a natural public speaker. None of us were. And yet you probably hear regularly some version of 'just be yourself on stage', or 'be authentic', and 'speak naturally and from your heart'. While these phrases may be well meaning and aim to encourage, for many of us, the idea of speaking in public unleashes panic, anxiety and fear. We live in a world where communication is the currency we trade with. Speaking confidently and effectively can make the difference in your business and relationships. My aim with *Speak Easy* is to boost your chances of trading and performing at a whole different level, so thank you for choosing to learn and well done for selecting this book of tools and tips to enable speaking with ease.

For more than two decades I have taught and trained thousands of people around the world both one-on-one and in workshops to speak and perform in front of an audience and overcome their fears of public speaking. *Speak Easy* is my attempt to personally work with you as if you're my client in the room. Together we'll improve your speaking skills, encourage thought about your body language, your voice and the words that come out of your mouth when you make a speech, pitch for new business or have a job interview. *Speak Easy* will help you perform exceptionally in a meeting, make a memorable television appearance, give a rousing lecture, make your wedding vows unforgettable, deliver a poignant eulogy and powerfully present to clients.

You are capable of giving life-changing speeches that give people hope and show them they can make different choices. You can pierce the hearts of your listeners by being brave and speaking from a place of sincerity. As American author, poet and activist Maya Angelou once said,

'I've learned that people will forget what you said, people will forget what you did, but people will never forget how you made them feel.'

Every day we present ourselves and people judge us based on how we do it. In following my practical advice in *Speak Easy* you can learn to be more confident and bold when taking centre stage or at the front of a room. I'll show you how to see insecurity as an exciting opportunity to transform your life and work. In trusting yourself you'll begin to see the power in taking risks, especially when you make yourself vulnerable in front of an audience.

The Greek word 'charisma' means 'state of grace'. Imagine if you were described as having that dynamic quality when you spoke. And imagine the possibilities that could open up for you if your words could reach that level of inspiration.

Speak Easy offers tips and strategies to embolden the unique style and presentation technique that lives in every one of us. You may choose to delve in and out of different pages and chapters or prefer to read it from cover to cover. There's no right or wrong way to use this book but I encourage you to always refer to it before presenting. Keep it in your briefcase or on your desk. It should be your constant companion and secret weapon before fronting an audience, enabling you to connect authentically as you stand up proudly and tell your story.

American poet, lecturer and essayist Ralph Waldo Emerson wrote, 'To be yourself in a world that is constantly trying to make you something else is the greatest accomplishment.' It takes a lot of courage to be yourself and allow people to see you warts and all. But in all my years taking stages, leading forums and making speeches I promise you that the most potent sort of presenting is when you make yourself vulnerable, speak about what makes you feel afraid and share your truest self with your audience. By revealing what you perceive as your failures as well as your triumphs when speaking publicly, people identify with you immediately. You are sharing what it is to be human and allowing honesty into the relationship between speaker and listener. That packs a powerful punch and may even inspire a standing ovation.

The publication of the first edition of *Speak Easy* in 2003 represented my debut as an author. I could never have dreamed or imagined I would have revised this book four times for publication in six countries. I have learned that if you write a good practical book that helps people it will have a long shelf life and reach more corners of the globe.

This latest edition has been thoroughly updated and it reads almost as a whole new book because I have grown in my professional and personal capacity thanks to clients who keep me inspired and challenged. It also needed rewriting because the world in which we live and work has been so radically altered with the advancement of technology. But the basic learning of the craft of public speaking is still a necessity if you want to progress in your career and be more persuasive.

I never get tired of receiving an email or a phone call from a stranger asking me to create a miracle for them before they give a keynote speech or a presentation. It's the beginning of a confidential and precious business relationship that often results in friendship. Helping people shine in a job interview, in a webcast film or on the business stage opens new doors and conquers new horizons. It's truly rewarding work that enables me to 'dwell in possibility' as American poet Emily Dickinson once wrote. She also wrote, 'If your Nerve, deny you — Go above your Nerve'. These are powerful words that reflect my personal creed.

I have been privileged to witness a transformation in so many people's lives as they overcome the fear of speaking publicly and step up to being the best version of themselves. My profession as a teacher, coach and trainer is one I cherish and in writing this book I hope to communicate how passionately I believe we can all live, work and speak to our fullest potential. In what seems like a lifetime ago, I trained as an actress in professional theatre. This experience taught me how to connect with people so they are drawn to you. It's not just about learning your script. It's about delivery and understanding that you are giving a performance even if you are talking in a meeting around a table.

It doesn't matter who you are or what you do, you will be called upon to speak in front of an audience at some stage in your life, especially at work. Why not make it memorable and even life altering? Why not give people hope and inspiration as you share who you are and what you know? Why not seize the imagination of your audience and be a rousing force for change? And yes, rehearse, rehearse and rehearse until you are extraordinary. You will thank me for this advice!

The longest serving First Lady of the United States, Eleanor Roosevelt, put it better than I ever could when she said, 'You gain strength, courage, and confidence by every experience in which you really stop to look fear in the face ... You must do the thing you think you cannot do.'

So, step onto centre stage. The curtain is about to open. Find the courage to be yourself. And *Speak Easy*.

With love,
Maggie xx

1
Confidence

'Risk anything! Care no more for the opinion of others ... Do the hardest thing on earth for you. Act for yourself. Face the truth.'

— Katherine Mansfield, *Journal of Katherine Mansfield*

You can overcome your fear of public speaking. There are role models of all races, ages and backgrounds — I see them every time I run a workshop.

This book is a goodie basket of information, stories and tips to help you to become a better public speaker and a confident communicator. Throughout this book I'll share my story and the stories of clients, friends and family who have conquered their fears and gone on to become accomplished and memorable speakers. Open up a new frontier for yourself as a person with presence. Learn from them.

Speak Easy is for everyone not just a business audience. While you may never need to give a formal speech, you can use your speaking skills in a variety of ways from informal meetings to Skype presentations and team events. My clients range from gang members to children, high performance athletes, customer service staff and chief executives of international corporations. *Speak Easy* is for people who want to improve the way they communicate — whether at a job interview, a wedding speech or a funeral, we all need to speak in public at some stage in our lives. I earn my living teaching presentation skills and yet this used to be my number one fear. Now, my job is helping people shine on the stage — that stage can be anywhere from a church to a boardroom or a Skype presentation to an overseas client.

My company, Fresh Eyre, can turn its hand to a variety of presentation courses but our most popular by far is: Creating Presence. It works because participants have two days to practise their speeches in front of a supportive audience while being filmed. People get to see themselves on video, get constructive feedback from us and from their peers, and see the struggles and vulnerability of others. Quite quickly they lighten up, have a laugh, play like children and push themselves to perform in ways they never imagined. This is as much a communication course as it is a presentation workshop that encourages people to discover an 'inner performer'.

On every course we see clients go from zero (confidence) to hero — finding the courage to perform and enjoy themselves along the way. I know it's not easy stepping outside your comfort zone. The good news is that many have gone before you and proven it's not only possible, but also exciting, inspiring and sometimes life changing.

What is confidence?

To develop confidence we need to trust ourselves and our audience. Believe it or not, very few audiences want a speaker to fail! Your self-esteem will increase when you take risks and are bold. Trust in your message — you are worth listening to!

As former US First Lady Eleanor Roosevelt famously said, 'No one can make you feel inferior without your consent.'

I often use this quote in my teaching and know that when people are brave and commit to improving their public speaking skills their confidence grows every time they do it. Sooner or later they say they actually enjoy it. Take every opportunity to speak in public, whether at a family gathering, a farewell function, graduation or prize giving.

Feel the fear and do it anyway

> 'According to most studies, people's number one fear is
> public speaking. Number two is death. Death is number

two. Does that sound right? This means, for the average person, if you go to a funeral, you're better off in the casket than doing the eulogy.' — Jerry Seinfeld, comedian

I've tried to find the original source for this quote with limited luck. However, when I use it in a speech, I get a laugh. Even though it's a gross exaggeration it seems to ring a bell!

Interestingly, I found the quote in the 1977 edition of *The Book of Lists* by David Walley Chinsky, *The Fourteen Worst Human Fears*. It claims that while 41 per cent of people feared speaking in front of a group, only 19 per cent feared death. Clearly this generated a really good script line for Jerry Seinfeld! It reminded me of my days in the theatre when we talked about 'dying out there' as a kind of shorthand for stage fright.

While it's nonsense to think anyone would choose death over giving a speech, fear is a natural reaction to public speaking and there's nothing wrong with you if you feel it, sometimes quite acutely. You can still be persuasive even when you're terrified inside; what you need is courage, strategies to help, and lots of practice to build your confidence.

We spend so much of our lives communicating in public — it's strange and interesting that we make so little investment in getting it right. The enemy of a good speech is far more likely to be lack of preparation and practice than nerves, so start by getting your content right and pay less attention to your nerves.

The *Oxford English Dictionary* defines fear as 'an unpleasant emotion caused by the threat of danger, pain or harm' and the *Macmillan Dictionary* defines nerves as 'worried feelings that make you afraid that you will not be able to do something well'. Preparation of good content and practice are both great antidotes for these terrible twins.

> **'It's not the Mountain we conquer but ourselves.'**
> — Sir Edmund Hillary, mountaineer, explorer

Great speakers weren't born that way; they learn a craft and eventually it comes naturally. Orator and historian Winston Churchill didn't start out as a skilled writer or speaker, but he topped his political career with a Nobel

Prize for literature and was the first person to be made an honorary citizen of the United States. For me, his famous quote sums it up, 'Success is not final, failure is not fatal: it is the courage to continue that counts.'

None of the skilled speakers you've observed, known or admired started out as superstars — they've had to learn how to speak in public, just the same as you.

What are we afraid of?

'I was embarrassed. I could feel my nerves curling like bacon over a hot fire.' — Margaret Halsey, author

Before every training session or workshop we send pre-course question-naires out to clients to help us design a programme to suit their needs. One of our questions is, 'What are your fears when speaking?'

Here is a list of the most common responses.

- They will judge me.
- Not being interesting.
- Not getting the message across.
- Fear of being nervous.
- Fear will reflect in my confidence.
- Worrying about what others think of me.
- Fear of forgetting my words.
- Fear of large audiences.

Over the years our clients, whether university graduates, managers, exec-utives or people who find themselves speaking at funerals or weddings, give the same reason for disliking public speaking: they are afraid of rejec-tion; afraid of losing their way and feeling out of control. They dread getting stuck for words during a speech; they fear negative feedback. I know I certainly used to feel this way.

Recently I asked one of my clients what she wanted to achieve in a session with me. 'I want to feel, and look like a rock star,' she replied. I just love that! On stage a rock star exudes confidence even if they're naturally shy.

When clients start working with me I talk to them about their childhood years and ask questions about when they first remember dreading speaking in front of a group. There's often a specific event or time when they felt embarrassed in public. This incident, which often seems insignificant, remains fresh in their mind. The important thing is to accept that the past is the past, and to see each day as a new beginning.

Naked in front of an audience

Imagine you're fifteen, standing on a stage waiting for the biggest performance of your life, when someone behind you accidentally stands on your trousers and your pants fall down? Your drama teacher is in the audience glaring, your parents have come to see their precious teenager perform and all eyes are on you.

When Claire, a senior businesswoman, came to me for coaching, she recalled the story as if it were yesterday, saying she wanted to shrivel up into a tiny ball and disappear. It has taken tremendous courage and coaching for her to overcome her fear of speaking to a large audience, but now she's a spontaneous and interesting speaker. Her solution to combat her dread of public speaking was to get out there and do it.

> *'Everything is a story. The mind spins stories out and you believe what the mind tells you. Every time you are stressed out or fearful you are believing what the mind is telling you.'* — Byron Katie, speaker and author

Why do we sometimes lose our inner sense of confidence in adulthood? I think it's frequently a result of criticism, negative feedback and a lack of encouragement earlier in life. Like elephants, we frequently hold onto memories of when something went wrong.

Facing the fear

We overcome fear by looking at it or facing it, whatever it may be. Pretending it doesn't exist is a sure way to make sure it does!

Remember that professional actors don't perform without learning their lines. Professional musicians must first learn to play their instruments. Professional speakers don't start out feeling confident about their presentations. They practise, learn their lines, discipline themselves and manage their nerves in front of an audience every time they perform.

Have courage

> *'If you want to conquer fear, don't sit home and think about it. Go out and get busy.'* — Dale Carnegie, writer and lecturer

You are not alone if you're struggling with a lack of confidence. Start talking about your memories while reading this book. You'll be amazed to hear other people's stories — hopefully they'll make you realize we're all the same.

You can improve your confidence by practising and increasing your knowledge about how to present. Eloquence is something you learn. Learning self-confidence in public speaking is no different from learning to play a musical instrument or a sport.

When I climbed the Himalayas with two girlfriends and a team of sherpas, I had zero confidence and tried to get out of it at the last minute. There was no turning back once I'd arrived in Nepal. I felt sick to my stomach ... my worst fear was that the sherpas would end up carrying me half way down the mountain. I'd worked with a personal trainer before the expedition, but climbing to well over 30,000 feet required courage. Making a speech or giving a business presentation may feel like climbing a mountain, but focus on one step at a time and the exhilaration of success will stay with you forever.

Here are some ideas for improving confidence in your public speaking.

Believe in yourself

The audience will believe you if you show them you're confident and comfortable in front of them. To appear confident you need to believe in yourself and in what you are saying. Be positive. Affirm yourself — gather a record of successful experiences. Tell yourself you are worth listening to and enjoy the moment when the audience applauds.

Share your stories and values

Don't play it safe — empower your audience, stimulate change in the minds of your listeners. No one else has your story, so be courageous and share it — make it the best it can possibly be. If the audience can relate to your anecdotes they'll connect with you and may even take away new strategies to help them deal with their own lives.

Prepare in advance

Procrastination is a killer. Take time to research your speech and do your homework. Do a little every day, even if it's just jotting down a few notes. Leaving preparation to the last minute will make you stressed and this is a sure way to reinforce your existing fears. If you're procrastinating ask yourself why. Have you put the speech in the too-hard basket? If your excuse is you're too busy, why did you agree to give the speech in the first place? If you are too busy to prepare properly (and it's not just an excuse) ask someone else to do the speech instead.

In *The People's War: Britain 1939–1945* Angus Calder says Winston Churchill took six to eight hours to prepare a 45-minute speech. Serious speakers need to allow 45 to 60 minutes of preparation time per minute of speaking time. I spend at least one to two full days preparing for a one-hour speech, and once spent four months preparing for a major speech, including practising in front of a friend to increase my confidence.

Fake it 'til you make it

If you're lacking in confidence, pretend you're not; project confidence even if you don't feel it. Move and stand with poise even if you feel awkward. Show your confidence to your audience through both your voice and your body language. After a while you'll start to feel like the confident person you're pretending to be.

While I was working in London, a client approached me through my website. She was suffering from severe anxiety attacks prior to and during business presentations. She had successfully managed to avoid speaking in public for years but had decided it was time to face up to her fears. She approached her boss, who supported her by making an investment in training.

I was astonished to see how much presence she had in her first session, even though she couldn't see it herself. She was subconsciously putting on a great act, even though she was terrified inside. Now she believes in herself and she is able to give presentations with more courage and confidence. Even though she's now a general manager she still manages her nerves with breathing techniques and positive self-talk.

Inspiration is everywhere

American keynote speaker Dr John Demartini visits the United Kingdom frequently. I've attended one of his workshops and seen him speak three times in London. He was born with a birth defect and lacked confidence as a child. A teacher told him that he would never read or write because he had dyslexia and a speech impediment. Watching talent like him live or on the internet is a great way to get inspiration. We all have setbacks in life and John is a shining example of what's possible.

As American football coach Vince Lombardi says, 'Practice doesn't make perfect, perfect practice makes perfect.' If you want to be remembered, heed his advice.

Here's what entrepreneur Richard Branson has to say on the subject, 'I realized that if I was going to be the face of our brand, I was going to have to talk the talk. What I soon learned was that practice made all the difference. The more prepared I was, the less I stammered and stumbled. Good speakers aren't just talented or lucky — they work hard.'

Know your key messages

What do you want your audience to remember and take away from your speech? Write them down, find stories and examples to go with them and memorize them. Know your material inside out. Remember you are the expert of your own story. Keep things simple and be concise. Be aware of the perils of over-researching.

Rehearse

Have a complete run-through. A rehearsal is vital for your self-confidence. A good rehearsal should include a good warm-up to make your body feel more alive. Sing, dance, practise tongue twisters or go for a walk. Practise for the big day — think of mastering your speech as you would approach learning a sport.

It's quite simple: if you don't rehearse, your speech will be a five or six out of ten, and if the unexpected happens and you haven't prepared for it — it might be a one or two! My business partner Allie Webber works from her own home office and the following is her practice formula.

'Once I've researched, written and edited the speech, I double-space it and print it out in 16 point. If Maggie's available I read it to her on the phone and get her invaluable coaching. I notice where I trip up on words of phrases. If it's a eulogy I notice where my own words make me cry and give myself time and space to deal with my sadness.

'After this first run-through I re-edit, smoothing out the problem areas and rephrasing things I know will make me crack up on the day. Next, I set myself up in the living room and read it to my husband or my next-door neighbour. Once I've had feedback from them I make more changes and then I practise the speech several times on my own. I push myself to project and deliver it as I might on the day. It helps that I live beside the sea … the ocean makes a great audience.

'This technique has stood me in really good stead, helped me get through some very tough speeches including several eulogies for very close friends.'

Find opportunities to practise

Don't wait for 'the big one' to practise your public speaking. Experiment in presentations where you're relaxed about the outcome, then you'll be better equipped to handle the big speeches.

Sometimes I suggest business clients practise in front of university graduates. Allie Webber calls these 'warm bath opportunities'; they are safe places, where you can get instant feedback to help to build your confidence.

Create a support team

All you need is one person to coach you, commit to your journey and be available to watch you rehearse and give you constructive feedback; even better if you can initiate a group.

We've been delighted to see a number of groups we've trained pick up this principle really brilliantly. After two days on creating presence, many of them have taken on the art of giving and receiving constructive feedback and know how to critique themselves and others really well. They know they will only keep learning and improving if they practise, so someone steps forward and offers to co-ordinate a workplace support group where they can meet to practise upcoming speeches and presentations.

Study the stars

There are a lot of famous personalities that used to be afraid of public speaking. Richard Branson is an example: while he comes across confidently on television, as a child he struggled with dyslexia. Research his profile and you'll be amazed to see you are not alone.

The award-winning TED talks provide a massive repository of video lectures, none of them much longer than 20 minutes. This is a great place to watch star performers on almost any topic you can imagine. It's also a great place to get inspired and learn new skills. Have a look on the www.ted.com video site.

TIPS ON DEVELOPING SELF-CONFIDENCE

- Plan and prepare well in advance. Take time to research and do your homework. Preparation shows you are committed.

- Share stories that will change other people's lives. Don't play it safe. Tell your story. People remember anecdotes. Paint pictures for your audience.

- Hold onto the memory of the last successful speech you gave. Focus on that positive experience, not the one that you associate with failure.

- Inspirational speakers. Watch TED talks before you write your speech to inspire you and get your mojo going.

- Believe in yourself. You are unique. There is no other you. The audience will believe in you if you believe in yourself. Speak positively to and about yourself.

- Know what your key messages and stories are, write them down and memorize them.

- Rehearse in front of a colleague, friend or a supportive team. Have a complete run-through. A rehearsal is vital for your self-confidence. If using PowerPoint or other technology make sure you rehearse with a colleague and do a full technology rehearsal. Film your performance and play it back.

- Remember rehearsals are equally important when using technology such as Skype, FaceTime, and phone conferencing.

- Remember when using social media such as Twitter, Facebook, LinkedIn, Instagram, and YouTube that it's also important to present yourself professionally.

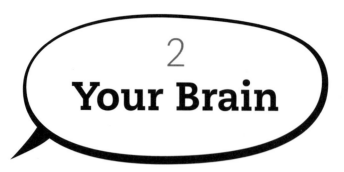

2
Your Brain

'While awake, a human brain can generate enough energy to power a light bulb.' — H.P. NEWQUIST, AUTHOR

The brain is your body's control centre. If you look after it and understand how it functions you can help it to work better, and your public speaking and general wellbeing will improve as a result.

According to the experts we only use about 5 per cent of our brain on our usual day-to-day tasks. What do we do with the rest? We use it to focus, think and communicate, so it's important to understand how to use it to its full potential. Imagine how much more you could achieve when writing or delivering speeches if you could only harness a little more of that latent brainpower.

As an actor I was more afraid of my mind going blank and forgetting my lines than anything else. Practise some of the exercises in this chapter and you will start to feel more focused and confident.

What is stage fright?

'Your mind will answer most questions if you learn to relax and wait for the answer.'
— William S. Burroughs, novelist and performer

Why could you remember your material when practising at home, but not when you went to give your presentation? Extreme fear or stress induced by being in front of an audience can trigger a chemical process in your brain, affecting your memory. This happens to many people when they give a presentation or speech.

Going blank

Journalist Giulia Sirignani has worked for the Australian Broadcasting Corporation and Channel 9 for over fifteen years, and for her it wasn't a real audience that triggered a blank, it was an estimated television audience of a million people. She'd been doing live reports from the Vatican in Rome three times a day for months to cover the death of Pope John Paul II. She and the network were happy with her performance and her self-confidence and esteem were in good shape. Then disaster struck.

'It was the day after the world learned that Joseph Ratzinger had been elected the next Pope. I was asked to do a live introduction to my story on the evening news. While I was waiting at the Vatican for the newsreader to introduce me, I suddenly started to get really, really nervous. I was extremely tired after months of very little sleep and felt distracted by movement on the set around me. Hearing my countdown from the studio in Sydney: 'ten, nine, eight, and seven ...' my heart started to race and, for no apparent reason, I felt terrified. I'd been working for television, doing this every day, for nearly fifteen years, so why the sudden panic attack? I started to talk, but heard a noise off-camera and at that point went completely blank and forgot what I was saying. It was the lowest point in my career. All attempts at consolation and assurances that "it happens to everyone" failed to move me. I still shudder when I think of the longest three seconds of my life!'

> 'It is natural to be nervous, but it is an art not to show it.' Laurence Olivier, actor

What causes stage fright?

In the *Brain Encyclopedia*, American author Carol Tarkington explains: 'An active human brain can generate 10 watts of electricity and weighs approximately 1.4 kilograms [3 pounds]. There are more than 100,000 chemical reactions triggered in the human brain every second.'

Dinah Bradley, author, international speaker and co-owner of Breathing Works, offers additional context, 'Our visual sense operates mainly in the larger area of the brain. No one has worked out why, but our brains don't differentiate between vividly imagined events and real ones. When you think about a painful or frightening situation, your body reacts as if it's actually happening.'

Experiencing stage fright is normal. Stay calm, breathe deeply and the words will come. Don't judge yourself. What seems like a lifetime to you is a few seconds to the audience. A good strategy is to ask them to help you. If I lose my words when teaching, I often say, 'Where was I now?' or I turn to my co-presenter and ask for help. Trust that someone will rescue or assist you — people want to help. They are on your side, don't want you to fail and may not even be aware of your mental block.

The stress reaction

Dr Gail Radcliffe is a clinical psychologist who has trained and worked in New Zealand and the United States for many years. She is a specialist in stress, depression, bullying, burnout, physical and emotional abuse, phobias, Obsessive Compulsive Disorder, trauma and anxiety-related disorders. Here she describes the changes that happen in your brain and body when you experience stress as a four-stage cycle.

1. Negative thoughts arise, such as 'I'm too scared to give this speech.'

2. Emotions, such as anxiety, arise from the negative thoughts.

3. Negative thoughts create chemical reactions in your body, which send nerve impulses to the adrenal glands at the top of your kidneys. This activates a number of different organs triggering the release of stress chemicals into your bloodstream interfering with neural transmission and making it harder for the brain to understand the messages it receives.

4. Physical symptoms like sweaty palms, a churning stomach or thumping heart occur. Symptoms can also manifest in

the brain, dilating the arteries, causing headaches and making it difficult to think clearly and remember things.

I have tremendous respect for experts like Dr Gail Radcliffe and Dinah Bradley and have often recommended that clients work with them. You can find experts in these fields in your city. Make sure you do your research and find someone you feel you can work with or get along with.

The effects of stress

Adrenaline is a hormone secreted by the adrenal glands that increases rates of blood circulation, breathing, carbohydrate metabolism and prepares muscles for exertion. If you are anxious or stressed before or during a speech, your brain is producing chemicals induced by fear, like adrenaline. When people feel they are in danger they experience a hormonal surge frequently referred to as an 'adrenaline rush'.

You've probably heard the expression 'fight or flight' used to describe the body's reaction to an extremely stressful situation. An adrenaline rush is okay in the short term because it gives you high energy, but it in the long term it can be dangerous and lead to burnout. I was diagnosed with it three times at the peak of my career, so can certainly verify how frightening and serious it can be. You may have experienced some of the following side-effects:

- heightened awareness
- increased respiration
- lightheadedness
- dizziness
- headaches
- changes in vision
- restlessness and irritability.

Fill out the burnout test in Chapter 14 on health and wellbeing and see where you sit.

When your brain is producing more adrenaline, it reduces the production of chemicals like dopamine and serotonin that help you feel relaxed and happy. A reduction in these two chemicals will lead to a lack of energy and motivation, and less positive thinking. I know I need them and think of them as my two happy travelling companions!

A deficit of serotonin can lead to depression. Serotonin, sometimes known as the happy chemical, is very important for maintaining: calmness, feelings of wellbeing and happiness, mood balance, appetite and sleep, and cognitive functions, including memory and learning.

Award-winning broadcaster and coach Clive Littin describes dopamine as 'nature's amazing motivator'. If you give a great presentation and get plenty of positive feedback you'll feel a dopamine rush. You'll feel good about yourself. When I finish running a workshop for my clients or give a dynamic presentation I experience dopamine going crazy in my system as part of the natural high. Dopamine is responsible for:

- feelings of pleasure
- feeling good
- helping you focus
- giving you some of your energy supply.

Following are some ideas to help you manage your adrenaline rushes and to reduce the effects of stress and boost your serotonin and dopamine levels.

EXERCISES TO REDUCE THE EFFECTS OF STRESS

BREATHING

Find a quiet place where you won't be distracted or feel inhibited. It could be in your hotel room or your office. Close your eyes for 5 minutes and sit with a straight spine. Take slow, deep breaths, focusing on the flow of breath in and out of your lungs. Relax your head, shoulders and arms. Let all the tension in your body go. Clear your mind of clutter. Visualize a gentle breeze taking away all the muddled thoughts preventing your mind from relaxing.

POSITIVE SELF-TALK

Say to yourself: 'I am calm, I am in control. I am ready to speak with ease.' Repeat this over and over, sending a positive message to your brain.

ASK FOR HELP

Call a friend or colleague you trust and ask for help. Ask them to listen to your presentation. I have many friends who phone, Skype or visit asking me for this kind of coaching. Even the process of putting the problem into words is a positive step. Talking about the issue is a constructive way to solve the problem, not an admission of failure.

CROSS CRAWLING

'Cross crawling' is a well-known accelerated-learning exercise and easy to do before a presentation. Tap your left hand to your right knee in front of your body and then repeat with your right hand and left knee. Next, repeat the sequence, this time with your arms and feet meeting behind your body. This exercise aims to integrate the left meridian of the brain with the right, which helps to relax your mind. You could think of a different activity that involves thinking and using both sides of your body — for example, you could juggle balls before a speech. It also takes your focus off your fear and gets the blood moving.

FREE THE BODY

- Stretch your arms out and have a big yawn.
- Shake your hands and feet to get the blood flowing.
- Check in to your body and see where the tension is. Is it in your shoulders, your face or your jaw?
- Tap and massage parts of the body.
- Imagine that you have a piece of chewing gum in your mouth and move your lips and chew — close your mouth and open your mouth.
- Hold your jaw with your thumb and forefinger and slowly open and close your mouth to relax your jaw.
- Use your favourite music to lighten your mood before a presentation. I often dance quietly on my own. It's a quick way to lose your inhibitions and free up your body.
- Boost your serotonin levels by going for a walk outdoors in the sunshine. A walk around the block can work wonders.

You could also consider getting organized early and walking to the venue where you're presenting.

RELAX

- Consider a massage on the morning of your speech.
- Turn your mobile phone off for a couple of hours.
- Have a bath, swim, shower or go to the hair salon and get your hair washed. Water makes you feel good and has a cleansing effect.
- No matter what time your presentation or speech is, there is always time to calm your mind and relax your body.

'There must be quite a few things that a hot bath won't cure, but I don't know many of them.' — Sylvia Plath, poet

LAUGH

- Boost your dopamine levels by visiting a friend who makes you laugh.
- Watch a funny movie or TV programme that will make you forget about your stress.

Looking after your brain

Look after your brain and you'll find speaking in public becomes easier because you're focused, alert and ready for action.

Oxygen

Lack of oxygen makes you drowsy and lethargic, and can cause memory loss. Have a window open if you can. Unfortunately many of us work in high-rise buildings with air-conditioning, so make an effort to leave the office every day to refresh yourself and get a good supply of oxygen to your brain. Oxygen helps you to think more clearly and you'll be more creative and engaged in meetings. Before you give an important presentation get some fresh air, even if you step outside for just a few minutes. Low levels of oxygen can also cause other symptoms such as light-headedness, nausea and fainting.

Restful sleep

Feeling nervous the night before a big presentation is completely normal. Getting enough sleep seems an obvious requirement, but it makes such a difference. We are more awake and positive when we get plenty of deep, relaxed sleep. Go to bed early the night before a big presentation. I'm a night owl, so I have to make a real effort to get enough sleep.

Clients often say they've stayed up late the night before a speech because they have left it to the last minute to prepare. If you're overtired, you won't be able to perform at your best. Restful sleep will help you much more than making last-minute changes or rehearsing until late the night before.

Founder of the Resilience Institute, Dr Sven Hansen, believes sleep could be the most important factor in our resilience. He says while well-being, exercise and nutrition get attention, there is a growing body of evidence that adequate sleep may be a key factor in reducing preventable disease and distress, and promoting wellbeing, emotional competence and cognition.

He suggests a sleep action plan could look like this.

- Prioritize sleep and aim for 7.5 hours with adequate cool-down time and a strict wake-up time.
- Avoid all screens and technology for 2 hours before sleep. (The science is unanimous on this.)
- A cool, dark and quiet bedroom is helpful.
- Use power naps to maintain afternoon productivity.
- Go to bed 90 minutes early to repay sleep debt at least once per week.

- Eat smaller evening meals.
- Try warming the body about 30 minutes before bed and then encouraging cooling. A cool shower, cool room, feet and hands outside bed covers and no electric blankets might help.

Brain food

The body needs fuel to energize you! Snack or 'graze' on brain food such as almonds, which are rich in protein, throughout the day. It is impossible for the brain to work without energy. You are what you eat. Salads and fruit are my favourite foods. I notice a huge difference when I eat more raw food. It keeps me mentally alert throughout the day. Most cafes offer fresh green smoothies and juices. If you don't have time to eat a full meal, buy a fresh green smoothie. This is great food on the go. If there is no way you can get lunch, at least have a banana close by.

I often see someone having a large piece of ginger crunch and several coffees before they perform. This massive caffeine and sugar hit will certainly add to anxiety and leave you feeling very speedy.

I'm also amazed at how many so-called high-performing professionals order up giant-sized muffins for morning and afternoon tea. My colleague Allie Webber reports a similar pattern and has quite a cute way of checking up on the 'eating culture' of clients she works with in media training. She says, 'Before we interview people we always do a sound check and ask what they had for breakfast. It's amazing the number of people who say they had a cup of coffee and a chocolate biscuit. It's often surprising to learn that some of them work in the health sector.'

If you eat good, clean, healthy food before you present you'll maintain your energy levels. Studies show that food intake is associated with an increase in blood levels of B-endorphins, an important vitamin for optimum brain function. Carrots are rich in vitamin B; take them to work to munch on. Aim to maintain a balanced diet by eating fresh food, including at least five portions of fresh fruit and vegetables every day. The brain needs nutrients just like other muscles in the body.

> 'One cannot think well, love well, and sleep well, if one has not dined well.' — Virginia Woolf, writer

Changing your eating habits will make an enormous difference to your energy levels and memory retention. I always believed it took 28 days to break a habit but research by health psychologist Phillippa Lally suggests it could take between two and eight months to build a new behaviour into your life, so best you get onto it quickly! If improving your diet is a new challenge, buy healthy snack food and carry it in your briefcase, handbag or pocket. Store it in an airtight jar on your desk and get into the habit of healthy snacking every couple of hours. You need energy to present.

Foods to boost your brainpower

If you are giving a speech in the morning or during the day a healthy breakfast is a must. Eat whole grains such as brown cereals and wheat bran. Include berries such as blueberries that are high in antioxidants and believed to be effective in improving memory, or blackcurrants that are rich in vitamin C and believed to increase mental agility.

If you are giving a speech in the afternoon eat oily fish for lunch with a salad — great for brain function! Good sources include salmon, trout, mackerel, herring and sardines. Some of the following foods are great brain food.

- Antioxidants found in tomatoes are good for the brain.
- Pumpkin seeds (pepitas) are good for memory and thinking skills.
- Broccoli improves brainpower and enhances cognitive function.
- Nuts are a great source of protein.
- Zucchini (courgettes) are rich in potassium and help lower blood pressure.

Fluids

If you do not drink enough water you may get a headache and feel exhausted. Make a habit of carrying a bottle of water with you so that drinking it becomes part of your routine, especially a week before your speech. The brain will tell you when you are low on fluids, so pay attention. The idea that we should all drink eight glasses of water a day is not necessarily scientifically accurate. But one thing's for sure: we need to drink enough! If you're giving a presentation or important speech, make sure you're well hydrated before the event. It will increase your energy and make a difference.

Keep coffee and tea to a minimum before speeches as they force your kidneys to excrete fluids from your body. I was so nervous when I first hit the speaking circuit that I drank endless cups of coffee in my hotel room beforehand and then wondered why I was speedy, headachy and always running to the loo! Now the first thing I do before a presentation is make sure I have a bottle of water on hand.

Never drink alcohol before a presentation or a speech. Nephrologist Dr Steven Guest says, 'Alcohol interferes with the brain and kidney communication and causes excess excretion of fluids which can lead to dehydration.'

Exercise

A brisk short walk before a speech or presentation will work wonders. Walking is a wonderful way of taking care of your brain. Most clinical psychologists recommend clients exercise to prevent burnout. We are nicer people to be around when we exercise because of the release of endorphins in our body. Endorphins are natural painkillers and elevate our mood, which is why we feel good after exercise.

It's easier said than done but try to make exercise a priority in your life — you'll appreciate the benefits. Attending a pilates, yoga or gym session first thing in the morning before your speech will make a difference.

Stimulate your brain

'Your brain can keep learning from birth till the end of life.' — Marian Diamond, University of California, Berkeley

The more you read, go to movies and plays, exercise, meditate, learn, study, write and partake in intellectual discussions, the more your brain is stimulated. Don't allow yourself to become bored with life or let your brain become lazy. It is an organ that needs feeding and stimulation.

Music and aromatherapy are both great for relaxation and enhancing your mood. My friends know that if they want to get me a present, the best gift they can give me is a luxury diffuser. I notice a number of corporates are now putting diffusers in their bathrooms and I really enjoy this when taking a break from teaching. Use music and aromatherapy in your office and home so it relaxes and calms you.

Music

Listening to music uses the whole brain, improves memory and will help you focus. It is also another great way to relax. Some specific music has a profound effect on your brain, your mood and wellbeing. I have a collection of relaxation music pieces that work wonders. While you're reading this put on your favourite music and notice how relaxed your body becomes.

Aromatherapy

Consider trying aromatherapy to help sharpen your memory skills — rosemary and basil essential oils are good for improving memory. Studies tell us that lavender increases alpha waves in the brain, which are associated with relaxation.

Spend some time researching what effect different aromatherapy oils have.

TIPS ON USING YOUR BRAIN

- Stress is a chemical reaction that occurs in your brain — learn to manage your stress by relaxing your body and your mind.

- Your brain is an organ that deserves to be looked after. Do all you can to care for it and keep it in good health. Mediate before a presentation.

- Your thoughts become reality. Think positive thoughts both before and during your presentation. Visualize a successful outcome to your speech.

- Communicating successfully involves quick thinking and energy to communicate ideas effectively to your audience. Paying attention to your health will help you to deliver a dynamic presentation.

3
Mastering Body Language

'Suit the action to the word,
the word to the action.'

— William Shakespeare, *Hamlet*, Act III Scene II

When did you last notice someone's awkward body language while they were giving a speech? Did it put you off? Was it distracting? I remember sitting through a 20-minute presentation where a senior manager stroked the inside of her thigh for the duration of the speech. I'm sure the speech was good but in the end that was all I remembered!

Your body language can tell the audience far more about you than you think — whether you're happy to be there, flustered or nervous. Whether you're presenting online, with technology or in person it frequently tells them far more than the words you actually speak. I'm a naturally animated and expressive speaker; I notice that my audiences respond to this, and get a sense of who I am. Become aware of your body language and make sure it carries the message you mean it to. This chapter will give you simple guidelines to help you communicate more powerfully and authentically.

When clients fill out our pre-course questionnaires some general concerns regarding body language include appearing wooden, overusing hand gestures, looking arrogant with hands on hips, and appearing nervous by absentmindedly bouncing. There can also be many other body movements that could distract an audience. A senior business development manager approached me for coaching because she was concerned that her uncontrollable tremor, due to nerve damage from intensive treatment for cancer, was noticeable. She had become very conscious of her shaking and fixated on it every time she had to give a presentation. This, in turn, worsened her shaking and had slowly eroded her confidence in speaking in public. She wanted me to help her find a way of getting through her nerves so her tremor was less obvious. After two days of working with her, she did the hard work by letting go of the anxiety. The more she relaxed and the less that she thought about her concerns, the more she performed with absolute passion — and succeeded.

These are the things I'm looking for in a good presentation:

- Eye contact — that's long enough and connects with all sections of the audience.
- A variety of appropriate expression and facial gestures.
- A variety of appropriate hand gestures.
- Appropriate warmth and smiling.
- Body language that indicates you are listening, relaxed and engaged with your audience.
- Excellent posture — both sitting and standing.

What the experts say

There are 750,000 body language signals of which about 1500 can be identified by facial movements and expressions alone. Emeritus Professor Albert Mehrabian from the University of California in Los Angeles is well known for his work on body language and non-verbal communication. His study, focused on the communication of feelings and attitudes, shows that 55 per cent of your message in these areas is determined by facial expression, 38 per cent is determined by the way your words are said (your voice) and only 7 per cent by the actual words spoken.

While 93 per cent of meaning, inferred by people in Mehrabian's study, came from body language and tone of voice, it's important to say that unless the speaker is talking about feelings or attitudes these equations do *not* apply. For example, the spoken instruction, 'Everyone evacuate the building because there's a fire,' carries 100 per cent of meaning in the words; that is, (1) there is a fire, and (2) get the hell out of here. You get the message fully through the words without having to be an expert on body language.

Gestures

Gestures are a natural part of human expression — it's fascinating to watch people from all over the world, particularly children, use gestures as part of their storytelling. In a study published in the 13 February 2009 issue of *Science,* University of Chicago psychologists Susan Goldin-Meadow and Meredith Rowe found that babies already showed a wide range of 'speaking' ability through gestures at fourteen months of age. They also found that children in different socioeconomic groups are socialized differently, with children from higher socioeconomic groups generally using more gestures to communicate meaning than children from lower socioeconomic groups. When they tested children at 54 months of age, those who'd used a variety of gestures early turned out to have better vocabulary than other students.

Facial expression

'The writing is important, but the way you say the line and the pause you give it, the facial expression — all of that is very important.' — Arnold Schwarzenegger, bodybuilder, actor and former governor of California

Dr Paul Ekman has had a long and distinguished career in psychological research and made a big contribution to our understanding of human emotion. He is best known for his work in the late 1960s when, with colleague Wallace Friesen, he studied the Fore people of Papua New Guinea and demonstrated the six universal emotions of happiness, anger, fear, sadness, disgust and surprise and their micro expressions. After this discovery, Ekman and Friesen went on to develop a tool for measuring any and all facial movements: the Facial Action Coding System (FACS).

These contributions benefit a broad range of fields, from animation to counter terrorism. FACS remains the gold standard for identifying any movement the face can make, free of interpretive inferences.

While these studies are fascinating and useful for people like me, for the vast majority of the population the messages they get about performing in public come from a set of behaviours they are frequently unaware of. Most people I teach have never seen themselves on camera and rarely had feedback on how they come across. Given so much of our time is spent in communication-related activities, we have an opportunity to not only observe other people's body language, but also to improve our own.

Why does body language matter?

It is much more interesting to look at somebody speaking if they are expressing themselves fully and using their body. Research suggests it only takes 30 to 60 seconds to assess someone after meeting him or her. Every time you deliver a speech or present in a meeting you are communicating non-verbally for some of the time. Make it a daily practice to observe people's body language, whether they are having a conversation on the street or using their mobile phone.

In one of our courses an elegant Croatian woman did not use gestures

when she was first filmed in a morning session. After watching her performance on the screen and giving her feedback, she had completely transformed by the afternoon. Often all it takes is some constructive criticism so people become aware of their body language. She was naturally expressive, so much so that the participants were sitting on the edge of their seats.

I often notice that when people think no one is looking at them, they're much more expressive with their gestures because they're not aware of an audience. In our work I frequently see people who are very animated, using gestures before the course starts, then turn into robots when they're in front of the camera or presenting to their peers. Invariably someone in the past has told them to control their hands and stop using gestures, and a number of people have taken this very seriously. Another classic is people who've been taught at school to look at the clock at the back of the hall instead of the audience. Others present with their arms folded over their chest or their hands in their pockets because that's what they see male sports stars do on television. This is closed body language.

You can learn to improve your body language

Few of us are born natural public speakers. We learn as we grow up and make mistakes; we learn from our families, our teachers, our upbringing, and from popular culture like the internet, television, magazines and advertising. We progress by getting constructive feedback, travelling, observing and asking. We improve with practice and by applying simple techniques. My artistic father was theatrical when he was expressing himself, so naturally I learned from him and many others along the way.

> 'Who you are speaks so loudly that I can't hear what you're saying.' — Ralph Waldo Emerson, writer

Feedback is crucial

The frustrating thing about trying to improve your body language is that it's very difficult to know how you come across unless someone gives you feedback. For example, you could wring your hands, play with your rings or sway while speaking. The beauty of our courses is that people get to see themselves on film and are able to see the habits for themselves. Sometimes we give the camera a name (Caroline is one) and tell the course that she is 'by far' the best trainer in the room! The common pattern is that people are so focused on delivering the words that the rest of the presentation goes out the window!

What to do with your hands

The most common thing that people say in our presentation skills workshops is that they feel uncomfortable because they don't know what to do with their hands. This generates a whole set of behaviour, most of which is neither flattering nor useful. We have a module on gestures and it includes a number of exercises in pairs that are very simple. We give people a phrase or sentence and each participant has to focus on three gestures that are relevant to the words. For example, if we use the phrase 'I speak from my heart', the gestures we often see are holding a hand to their heart, crossing both hands to their chest or pointing to their heart with one finger — rather than standing with their hands at their sides. During this exercise the participants give each other feedback. They enjoy having the opportunity to try out and experiment with an array of gestures using their faces and hands. It encourages them to think about the relationship between words and movements. You can easily practise this in front of the mirror or with someone at home when you're rehearsing your presentation. Remember, it's important to use natural gestures when you present your speech. Often a starting point is to send a message from the brain to the hands that it's OK to gesture! Being fully expressive can be quite heady stuff and it's exciting to see people, who arrived on a course using no gestures at all, using them to great effect by the time they leave.

In working with clients, we get them to observe their posture on screen so they can see for themselves when they are hunched up, lop-sided or looking awkward. As we review their performances on film, it's great to see the transformation from a crunched-up diaphragm and droopy shoulders, to chest out, spine straight, head sitting comfortably on top of the spine, looking 'on top of the world'. Sometimes it's a useful exercise to turn off the sound and simply study what you're doing with your facial expressions and the rest of your body. For example, a speaker saying, 'It's great to be here today' with his eyes glued to the page is actually saying the opposite through his body language.

People, who have never been to a presentation skills workshop or had any professional training, often start off with their legs or arms crossed (sometimes both). They not only look like they want to go to the toilet, but they look angry and set themselves up for a variety of unhelpful postures for the rest of the speech. We call this closed body language. The other thing we notice is people standing with their hands behind their back, which says, 'I'm nervous'. If you are investing in a coach to help you improve your confidence, make sure that they film you and play it back — otherwise you don't get to see your mistakes.

Basics of body language

Posture

We learn a lot about human beings by looking at their posture. If we hunch our shoulders and look at the ground we give the impression that we don't really believe in what we are saying. If we stand tall with our shoulders back, we appear confident. Avoid sitting and presenting, unless you have an injury, even if you're only presenting to five people in the room. We look more powerful if we are standing, it's more commanding and you have more authority to persuade and engage your audience. However, there are circumstances when it would be  appropriate to sit. For example, in my public relations days, I gave a series of communication workshops pro-bono to a group of teenage mothers, and chose to sit on the floor and talk with them because they were sitting on the floor. I wanted to 'get on their level' and didn't want to be intimidating. Use your judgment to decide. Many of my clients tell me they don't want to stand in a boardroom and give a presentation, but I insist on it and they always have a breakthrough. When standing up and performing, just think of your body as a puppet with a straight spine and the hands moving.

The biggest mistakes are: leaning to one side with your hip thrust to the side, hands crossed over your 'private jewels', standing with your bottom out when you're leaning over the microphone, and hanging on to the podium like it was about to take off in the wind. These all create an impression of nervousness.

'Maintaining good posture requires an awareness of ourselves.' — Dr Tristan Roberts, former leader in Physiology at the University of Glasgow

How you hold yourself physically can reflect how you think of yourself. How you think of yourself is usually how others will think of you. The audience tends to treat you exactly as you ask to be treated. For example, when we are happy we walk along the street with our heads up high and a smile on our faces. Our posture tells onlookers we are feeling good about the day. Standing straight also makes you feel more in control. It is my belief that communication and energy cannot be separated. Be conscious of what your body is saying and doing. Is it slumping saying, 'I am tired and exhausted?' Is it closed and defensive? Is it open and speaking to the audience with enthusiasm? Posture never deceives an audience. Your body tells the truth — it speaks to us.

Purposeful movement

Have your feet firmly on the ground, parallel with your shoulders. Be grounded and then move with a purpose; for example, walk across the stage while speaking to be closer to people on the other side. You don't want to be walking on the spot because it looks like you are restless and nervous. A common mistake people make is stepping out in front of them and stepping back or stepping to the side and back. You're not in a dance class! Remember, if you move too much you can hyperventilate because you're using up energy. There is also a real power in stillness. If you're being filmed for a company presentation, make it easier for the camera-person by telling them beforehand when you might move. That said, don't get too hung up about it and feel like you are glued to the spot.

People are often defined by the way they move. Characters in a play or a film are often directed to move in a certain way to portray a character. For example, John Wayne has a very distinctive walk and swagger that has been referred to many times over the years. Charlie Chaplin also had a unique walk: toes out, short steps and fast pace. I'm a fan of *The Graham Norton Show* and I was watching one episode with the Irish actor Jamie Dornan talking about how people often commented on his walk. A producer told him that he stepped on his tiptoes with a slight bounce. The producer then asked if it was a character trait or his normal walk; it was his normal walk. He was finally told to walk heel to toe and he said he'd never thought about it. When you're observing people moving notice if they're pigeon-toed or if they lean back. Pay attention to others and their movements and posture so you can learn about purposeful movements and how distinctive they can be. I use many exercises in our workshops to give our clients an opportunity to experiment with posture and walking so they can find out for themselves what feels comfortable and looks confident. Again, filming a rehearsal works well because you can see if you are swaying, pacing or shifting your weight from hip to hip. You can see if your movements across the stage are purposeful.

'Is there a John Wayne without that walk?'
— Ken Howard, actor

I often walk towards my audience to feel closer to them, speak and move back to what I call home base — centre stage or the lectern. If you sit or stand in one place for too long you can become stiff or rigid. Your audience will respond more if you are moving in a relaxed, coordinated way. Just remember you need a lapel microphone if you intend to move away from the lectern.

Move with grace, with your body truly connecting to your message. Meaningless or repeated movement doesn't add to your presentation and may even confuse your audience because the movement doesn't draw them into the narrative. Act out a character in a familiar story, experimenting with movement. Work in front of a partner, then act out the same story with inappropriate movements and analyze the effect this has on your audience.

Watch your friends and colleagues move at business functions, or family gatherings. Do they move with ease? Do they carry tension in their bodies?

Dr Geordie Jahner is an expert in teaching movement and teaches dance classes in America every year. She says, 'Movement, when explored consciously and with awareness, is an amazing tool for freeing the creative self and the creative imagination. By freeing the body, we automatically begin to free ourselves emotionally and mentally from the things that hold us back. A freely moving body exudes confidence and enthusiasm and allows the natural flow of our innate creative spirit. Our habitual postures, gestures and body language vividly reflect our internal states and communicate volumes to our audience. A stuck body equals a stuck self. A healthy moving body reflects a healthy moving self.'

EXERCISES TO ENCOURAGE NATURAL MOVEMENT

Before your presentation loosen up your body by doing one or more of the following:

- Running or walking on the spot.
- Shaking your feet or legs one at a time.
- Shaking your whole body.

Natural gestures

Gestures are usually defined as movements of the hand, arm, body, head, or face that express an idea, opinion or emotion. Every gesture should accentuate the points you are making, but not take away from them. Natural gestures highlight a point, influence the way an audience looks at you and listens to you. They are organic and flow from within when we're engaged in conversation.

> *'You cannot shake hands with a clenched fist.'*
> — Indira Gandhi

My first contact with clients is revealing because their handshake tells me if they're confident, shy or nervous? A soft, floppy handshake implies a lack of confidence. I have always encouraged my clients to discover their own vocabulary of gestures. Gestures help convey the message. They must be natural, expressive and clear. But they must also be spontaneous and authentic. Never use gestures for the sake of using them.

I never train people to use a particular pattern of gestures, because it appears false and robotic. The more you're comfortable and relaxed in your body and passionate about your message, the more natural gestures will follow. When you fiddle with a ring, touch your face or play with your clothing, you send out a message that you are tense, uncertain or not really focused on what you're saying. Your gestures must match your words, not contradict them. If you say something one way verbally but a different way non-verbally, your audience will always believe your non-verbal message.

EXERCISES TO ENCOURAGE NATURAL GESTURES
Before your presentation do the following:

* Shake your arms.
* Shake your hands and relax your fingers.
* Clench your hands and relax them, and repeat. Then lift your shoulders up, holding them tight and still. Next, drop them gently and relax. Repeat the exercise, being aware of your breath, breathing in as you raise your shoulders and exhaling as you lower them.

Practise delivering your speech walking around the room using gestures and then standing still but using your arms and hands. Which feels more natural?

Facial expressions
An expressionless face has no life; it simply looks as if you don't care enough to put the effort into delivering your message. If you're telling me that you are passionate about your work and your face is in neutral I don't believe you. Phoney smiles also give you away; a true smile comes from within. Of course, there are times when it's not appropriate to smile, so be aware of the context of your presentation.

EXERCISES TO RELAX YOUR FACE BEFORE A SPEECH
We wear our tension on the face, so do at least one of these to look and feel more relaxed.

- Try to touch your nose with your tongue.
- Slowly massage your face with your hands, with your eyes closed.
- Move your tongue around in your mouth, massaging the inside of the mouth.
- Open your mouth, stretching all the muscles, eyes wide open, then close your eyes and mouth, screwing your face up. Repeat then relax.
- Blow air between your lips, like a horse.
- Laugh — it's a great tension reliever.
- Splash cold water on your face to freshen yourself up or use a natural water spray.
- The tongue twisters in the warm-up chapter on page 112 will help to loosen up your face and jaw.

Eye contact

> '*I like you; your eyes are full of language.*'
> — Anne Sexton, poet

Eye contact is vital in good communication. It humanizes you and implies honesty. It shows you care and are interested in your audience, helping people to embrace your message and feel a part of your journey. An elderly friend of mine, who died in her nineties, always told me about a story of Laurence Olivier performing in a play in London in the sixties. She was in the audience and his eyes met hers when he walked onto the stage. She felt special and honoured, and felt as though he had connected with her.

> '*The eye is the window of the human body through which it feels its way and enjoys the beauty of the world.*' — Leonardo Da Vinci, artist and scientist

Looking into a person's eyes helps build a rapport with them. Looking someone in the eye is not intended to make them feel uncomfortable — don't stare, simply maintain eye contact for a few seconds at a time.

If the audience is too big for you to make eye contact with every person, try to make eye contact with at least a few people from different sections, including those at the back and sides of the room. When I performed at my first celebrity debate a journalist in the audience told me, 'You were wonderful but you hardly looked at the audience, you spoke to your notes too much.' The auditorium was in darkness, so I had almost forgotten there was an audience present. I was grateful for her honesty. Every time you make a mistake like this, celebrate it. You will move on and improve.

If you have never worked on a stage with lights in your face and the audience in the dark, get access to a studio and rehearse in this environment. Remember to avoid looking at the ceiling, floor and walls, and practise maintaining eye contact with people.

It is important to be aware of cultural differences. In some Asian and South American cultures eye contact is seen as disrespectful. This is also relevant to some Pacific Island cultures. I've seen some clients struggle to maintain eye contact with a small audience because it goes against everything they've been taught. Be careful not to jump to conclusions in a one-on-one meeting if somebody doesn't make eye contact with you all the time.

According to many body language experts, the normal number of blinks per minute is six to eight. The eyes are closed for a tenth of a second. When I am working with clients one-on-one I notice they blink a lot more than usual because they are nervous. This is where playback from the filming is important, as it gives people an opportunity to see it for themselves.

Here are some eye-contact rules:

- Never look down. Instead, maintain frequent eye contact whether you're listening or talking, but never stare.

- Embrace the audience with your eyes and keep your eyes up. Too much eye contact can give out the wrong signals such as flirting, anger or a challenge, so give some relief by looking away every few seconds.

- The 7-second rule works for most of my clients. Look for 5 to 7 seconds per person or per row then move your eyes on.

'The eyes are the window to your soul.'
— William Shakespeare, playwright

HINTS FOR HEALTHY EYES
- If you wear glasses or contact lens, make sure you have them with you when presenting and a back-up pair if necessary.
- Use drops in your eyes if they are sore.
- Put chilled cucumber slices on your eyes, and lie down for 5 minutes.
- Put a few drops of lavender oil on an eye pillow and place over your eyes, lying down for at least 10 minutes.
- Carry an eye mask in your briefcase and block off all light.
- Have a nap.

Common body language mistakes and nervous habits

Nervousness can affect your body language. Watch out for the following distracting mistakes that can diminish the power of your performance:

- Blinking.
- Twitching.
- Licking or chewing the lips.
- Picking you teeth with your fingernails.
- Touching your hair.
- Head tilted to the side.
- Touching your face.
- Chin resting on hands.
- Playing with your beard or stroking your chin.
- Jiggling one leg continuously when sitting.
- Crossing your arms or hugging yourself.
- Clicking a pen.
- Fiddling with your notes.
- Hands clasped behind back.

- Arms folded across your chest.
- Hands on hips.
- Hands nervously wringing or gripping.
- Hands in front of crotch (fig-leaf pose).
- Hands in pockets juggling coins.
- Playing with your ring or other jewellery.
- Adjusting your tie, belt, waistband or bra strap.
- Shuffling your feet, walking on the spot.
- Pointing your finger at the audience.
- Bouncing up and down on the balls of your feet.
- Standing with legs very wide apart.
- Staring at your feet or at the ceiling — avoiding eye contact with your audience.
- Shaking.
- Playing with your beard or stroking your chin.
- Hunching shoulders.
- Not smiling.
- Playing with glasses, taking them on and off, or pushing them up the nose.
- Lip and chin twitching.

TIPS ON BODY LANGUAGE

- **Face** — every time you deliver a speech you are communicating non-verbally with your face. Remember to smile and be expressive.

- **Eye contact** — keep eye contact with your audience and keep your eyes off your notes as much as you can.

- **Gestures** — gestures highlight the points you are making.

- **Posture** — stand tall with your shoulders back.

- **Movement** — needs to have a purpose.

- **Feedback** — get feedback to improve and film yourself to see what movements look natural and unnatural.

- **Study** — other people's body language so you increase your awareness.

4
Finding Your Voice

'The one thing that you have that nobody else has is you. Your voice, your mind, your story, your vision. So write and draw and build and play and dance and live as only you can.'

— Neil Gaiman, novelist, script- and screen-writer

D oors will open in all parts of your life when you sound confident and your voice is memorable. Your voice is unique and a big part of who you are. Read this chapter and challenge yourself to look at what you can do to develop your voice and project more powerfully.

We are judged by our voice in job interviews, speeches, business presentations, meetings and on the phone. I wasted too many years feeling upset about the sound of my voice when I worked as an actor. Voiceovers on radio were a way to earn extra money and I enjoyed being in a sound studio despite my lack of confidence. Acting in TV commercials also helped me hone my skills and pay the bills. However, I do look back at some of them and cringe!

Most clients and friends have told me that they don't like their voice. What often makes the difference is constructive feedback. I've had a number of excellent voice teachers in New Zealand, New York and the United Kingdom, and over the years I've overcome an initial lack of confidence and started to appreciate the way I sound.

Many clients tell us that attending a workshop has helped them learn about their voice and become more self-aware. It's also helped them think about tone and manner, the importance of breathing, pausing, changing pitch and the speed of delivery.

According to a fear-of-public-speaking study, undertaken by the National Institute of Mental Health, 70 per cent of people suffer from some sort of speech anxiety. This doesn't surprise me, given the thousands of emails I've received over the years from clients confiding their concerns and anxieties about their voices.

In hundreds of one-on-one coaching sessions I've heard how emotionally crippled people feel when they can't project their voice due to fear and nerves. There is so much you can do to improve your voice. I received the best voice tuition in my twenties as an actor at Theatre Corporate in Auckland. My two teachers, Linda Cartwright and Elizabeth McRae, were both top-class and helped me make a number of changes that have stood me in good stead all my life. I still have the odd refresher class with Linda and certainly turned to her when I had a guest role in a long-running television soap, *Shortland Street*, on a trip back home from the United Kingdom.

If you relax your body and learn to breathe correctly you will speak more confidently. Good posture helps you to breathe with ease and the tension in your body will disappear with practice.

Try some of these exercises and you'll discover that you not only have something to say but can also be more persuasive. The more you rehearse your speech the more at home you will feel with your sound.

The sound of your voice

You know immediately when someone is depressed, angry or unhappy from the sound of their voice. Traumatic events trigger all sorts of unpleasant emotions and this impacts the way we speak. After my mother died my voice often sounded flat on the phone and I felt drained of energy. Friends told me I sounded down. I wanted to be professional and pretended to be upbeat in business meetings, but close friends could tell the difference.

Improving confidence

We nearly always have a voice expert present in our programmes and with their help we witness people's lives transforming as they break through their old habits and patterns, and start to use their voices more fully. We have listened to senior businesswomen sound timid on the first morning of the programme, and by the second day, they sound powerful. By improving your inner confidence you will start to find and use your natural voice.

Everything is a choice

People who sound timid often lack credibility in the eyes of their colleagues. Social conditioning and our personal psychology both influence our voice, but we can learn strategies to alter these. All that matters when you are presenting is that people understand you. We have a choice about how we use our voice to express ourselves better. Very shy people often speak quietly as though someone has turned their volume down. Some of the most rewarding work I do is with people who have hidden behind shyness all their lives. If you want to be heard you need to speak up otherwise it is a strain for the audience. Some clients think they need a voice coach but on many occasions they just need an actor or presentation-skills tutor to take them through some theatre exercises so they can feel and see the difference when filmed.

The mystery and magic of language

There are now numerous hypotheses about how, why, when and where language might have emerged. Research suggests there's little more agreement on these questions today than there was 100 years ago, when Charles Darwin's theory of natural selection was being hotly debated. Suffice to say, since the early 1990s, a growing number of professional linguists, archeologists, psychologists, anthropologists and others have come up with new theories and ideas to what some consider the 'hardest problem in science', but none has arrived at a definitive answer.

What we do know is that humans use hundreds of muscles in the creation of sound and are born with a very precious brain, vocal equipment and genetics that have given us the unique ability to create the over 6500 languages spoken in the world today.

We start by imitating the accent and tone of our parents and are subsequently influenced by teachers, friends and the wider culture and environment we're brought up in. My father spoke quickly and so did I for many years until I had some training. Whenever I am in the presence of people with an accent I start to copy the way they sound. It's because I'm an actor. When I lived in Texas teaching movement to actors, I found I needed to slow down, adopt a drawl and enunciate my vowel sounds differently.

You can learn to sound more relaxed and confident by warming up your voice. It is worthwhile investing time and money in a qualified voice coach to build your confidence. If you decide to do further research into how to use your voice effectively, I recommend *The Right to Speak* by Patsy Rodenburg, who is based in London and teaches frequently throughout Europe and the United States. She has also written other books that will increase your understanding of this fascinating area: *The Need for Words, The Second Circle* and *Presence*. David Carey and Rebecca Clark Carey have written a useful book, *Vocal Arts Workbook and DVD; Body and Voice* by Marina Gilman is interesting if you want to delve deeply into this subject; and *Voice Work: Art and Science in Changing Voices* by Christina Shewell is excellent, although somewhat technical. There are many great books on the market, so ask around.

Passion

If your voice is flat and you're talking in a monotone you can sound depressed or bored. Regardless of how you actually feel, if your voice lacks variation of pitch and pace, you will not command attention. When we are happy we sound more passionate; we have zing and energy in our voice. Passion is not about technique, it's about enthusiasm and intense feelings — feelings that are hard to convey when you are stressed, tired or overworked.

> '*Be still when you have nothing to say; when genuine passion moves you, say what you've got to say, and say it hot.*' — D.H. Lawrence, playwright and poet

Practise reading a paragraph from the newspaper with energy in your voice, video it, play it back and experiment by emphasizing 'key' words. Inject enthusiasm in to your reading — go over the top and be theatrical to see how it feels and looks. I often do this when I'm coaching clients who lack animation. I demonstrate what I mean so they can imitate me. At first they are embarrassed when I ask them to present as though they are a circus ringmaster, but they soon realize that being larger than life is not over the top — it's simply more interesting. There is a performer in all of us. We just have to give ourselves permission to let it out.

Emotions

Your voice reflects your thoughts and feelings. Words by themselves are not enough; we need our audience to believe us.

I often tell clients to listen carefully to presentations on TED talks and watch television to discover what it is they admire about a particular voice.

People who express emotions in their voice move me. My closest friends are usually expressive, animated storytellers. They are often risk-takers, people who dare to share their inner selves without worrying about what other people think of them. There is a freedom in this. It's rare to see and exciting to be around.

> *'To free the voice is to free the person.'*
> — Kristin Linklater, vocal coach and author

At the 2015 World Cup Cricket semi-final, 40,000 people yelled, screamed and chanted watching the Black Caps play South Africa in Auckland. My brother Eddie and I watched the game on television and I was reminded of how excited human beings get when they are passionate about something. Towards the end of the game my voice was animated, as was Eddie's. We were gasping and holding our breath in anticipation. Why is it that we feel more inhibited in a business environment than we do watching an exciting, action-packed game? When the Black Caps won you'd think we'd both struck gold! We all need to bring this passion to our presentations.

Emotional issues often keep you stuck in old habits. In one course a client, who'd been raised in India, talked about how the culture influenced him to be 'very polite, quietly spoken and seen and not heard'. I gave him an impromptu exercise to tell his life story in 5 minutes and he realized it was far more engaging because there was enthusiasm behind the words. His work-focused presentation had been flat and lacking in enthusiasm. After seeing himself on video he noticed that his words needed to connect with his audience at an emotional level. After a number of regular weekly sessions he began presenting strongly and confidently and was finally able to project his voice in front of politicians, local government officials and professionals. He became aware that he didn't need to adopt a particular technique or style from anyone else and saw he was a much better presenter when he trusted his own voice. In summary, he gave himself permission to release his passion.

Learning from others

British celebrity chef Jamie Oliver uses a colloquial style and has made it part of his signature for success. He is a nice middle-class kid from Essex and he has adopted the London street-savvy accent, and you can certainly hear it in his voice. He uses groovy language and even borrows from other languages, like using the Hindi word 'pukka' which means 'cooked and ripe'. He is spontaneous and unstuffy and isn't trying to be something he is not. What makes him great is that he's unashamedly himself and uses that to make cooking accessible, healthy and exciting.

New Zealand voice teacher Linda Cartwright responded to my request to critique a 2015 Hillary Clinton speech. Read her critique and follow the link below to listen to the speech yourself. This will give you a focused, uninterrupted routine for studying people's voices on the internet. Imagine if you listened to one high-profile speaker every week and wrote down what you learned about their voice. What makes them interesting and compelling? Do they have perfect diction? Emphasize key words well? Do they pause for effect? Inject exuberance?

Hillary Clinton is probably one of the world's most experienced female speakers. She was a lawyer and an experienced performer before she even came to politics. She was First Lady for eight years, a US Senator for eight years and then served as Secretary of State for a further four years —

travelling to 112 countries and speaking frequently as part of her job.

Hillary Clinton YouTube clip:
https://www.youtube.com/watch?v= UH9rC0MaBJc

This is what Linda had to say:

TONE, PITCH AND DICTION:

- This voice is nicely centred, which means she is using both upper and lower harmonics in the tone.
- There is a fullness of tone and her voice sounds as though it is coming from the middle of her. It's authentic, which means who she is, is what you get, vocally.
- She's not trying to push her pitch range down — to sound more authoritative as some women in public life do. (This is because they know that male voices are traditionally allied with authority and they deliberately try to emulate them.)
- It's certainly the voice of a mature woman. It's not light in tone or in any way trying to appease her audience or bring out their protective instincts.
- All that information is carried not only on her tone quality, but also the words she chooses and the way she communicates as a whole. She is fluent, articulate and engaged.
- She has a reasonable pitch range and her diction is clear, so the voice is easy to listen to and what she's saying is easy to understand.

PASSION, POSTURE AND CONFIDENCE:

- She speaks with passion but doesn't get shrill and out of control; her arguments are considered and valid; she is courteous without trying to appease.
- In the performing arts, people are trained to stand with an aligned body, so they can stand and be observed by others without fear, without having to apologize for themselves and without aggression. Their voices must mirror this so that they express themselves fully without fear, without apology and without aggression. This is a woman who knows her own mind and is not afraid to speak it.

The King's Speech

One of my favourite movies is *The King's Speech*, the story of King George VI and his struggle with speaking in public. The movie has such a powerful message about speech impediments and stage fright. King George had a chronic stutter but he worked with his coach, Lionel Logue, and it transformed his life. During the time of his reign, it was considered shameful that a king lacked confidence when speaking in public. We are lucky that we live in a time where there is no stigma attached to seeking this kind of professional help. If you haven't seen this movie, watch it and you'll be inspired by one man's courage under the influence of an experienced teacher. Not only did King George overcome a speech impediment but he also found his own true voice. You can too!

Accents

Teaching clients about accents is some of my most challenging work because it involves undoing years and years of deeply ingrained habits about the way we view ourselves. Everyone has an accent. As a New Zealander I've had the experience of not being understood when travelling overseas. According to other English speakers, we often speak too quickly, pronounce words incorrectly, and our vocal expression is clipped and disconnected from expressive body language. This can make it difficult for those who speak English as a second language to understand us. We need to be patient, listen to people from other cultures, and watch the way they express themselves. Tune your ears to different ways of speaking. Be patient and really listen when people with accents are speaking. We all want to be heard. Encourage people for whom English is a second language to be brave, speak out and participate.

> *'You can speak influentially and well in any accent.'*
> — Judy Apps, professional voice coach

Preparing your voice

It is important to prepare your voice and body before a presentation. Before you jog you stretch — apply the same principle to your voice. The voice is your instrument and needs to be maintained so that you don't damage it. Stress, stage fright, tiredness and emotional trauma all have a negative effect on your voice. Never speak without warming up your voice first. (See Chapter 8 for a full warm-up programme.)

EXERCISE

A useful exercise to prepare your voice before presenting is called 'The Greeks', which we teach in all of our presentation-skills programmes. The exercise focuses on using vowel sounds, A E I O U, to help prepare the voice and body for a presentation. Each vowel sound has its own movement, which also helps to focus the mind. Practise the exercise in one fluid motion.

1. Stand up straight and breathe in deeply. The entire exercise occurs during an exhalation of one breath.
2. As you exhale say the letter A with your arms by your sides and your palms facing outwards.
3. Say the letter E and move your hands into a fig-leaf pose, below your stomach, with your palms facing your body. One hand on top of the other.
4. Say the letter I while lifting your right arm up to the side as if reaching for the sky and your left arm reaching toward the ground. Bend your right knee and straighten your left leg so it's parallel to your left arm.
5. Say the letter O while moving your arms in towards your body to create a circle in front of you, with your fingertips touching. Your knees should be bent softly and your feet firmly on the ground.
6. Say the letter U while bringing the heels of your hands together then lifting them in an 'offering' gesture.

This is a useful exercise before you give a team pitch. It may feel uncomfortable at first but you will start to concentrate more as you repeat the exercise at least three times.

Body alignment

It is important to pay attention to your body alignment because your posture and balance can affect the sound of your voice. Good body posture is essential for a good voice. The alignment should feel confident, regal and/or noble and be accompanied by an inner sense of balance and poise.

Good body alignment looks like this:

1. Keep your knees loose and relaxed. Check that you are not locking your knees or bending them too much. Keep your feet slightly apart at shoulder width with your weight evenly spread over both feet.

2. Make sure your spine is elongated and that your head is balanced on the top of your spine. The back of your neck will feel long and your face will be parallel with whatever wall you are facing. This simply means that you're not jutting your chin forward or tucking it down and looking at your audience from under your eyebrows, the way the very shy young Princess Diana used to do.

3. Make sure that your hips are aligned with your spine and shoulders. Women, particularly, often sit down into their pelvises, which doesn't allow the spine to lengthen and inhibits the breathing process.

4. Check that your shoulders are relaxed, your rib cage is lifted up and out and that you're breathing deeply — a dead giveaway of nervousness is when a speaker's shoulders are up around their ears or their body curls in to themselves.

5. Check for tension around the mouth and particularly the jaw — jaw tension is extremely common and affects both clarity and tone.

EXERCISE

Imagine a piece of string running through the centre of your head, down the back of your neck and spine. Now imagine it lifting you up through the top of your head, causing your spine to straighten. Ensure your weight is evenly spread over both sides of your body. Turn your head gently to the right, then return to centre, then left, then return to centre. Repeat 10 times.

Breathing

We are notoriously lazy about our intake of breath and it is very common to find people constantly allowing air into only the top of their lungs. This means the voice lacks depth and often sounds tense.

EXERCISE

Practise breathing through your nose not your mouth. Close your mouth and take three deep breaths to the bottom of your lungs. (When we speak we take air in through our mouth as well, otherwise it would take forever.) Huff all your breath out without collapsing the body and what is called the 'elastic recoil' of breath will take place. You can aid this by releasing your belly, as though everything from your waist drops down to the pelvic floor, the instant you know the breath is going to come in your body.

Diction

Articulating means pronouncing your vowels and consonants clearly. There's not much point in giving a brilliant speech if you can't be understood.

When we send out pre-course questionnaires we ask clients to tell us their greatest weakness when communicating. One senior manager who is a confident presenter shared, 'Mispronunciations have a way of side-tracking my delivery. Do I ignore them and move on or do I play on it and work it in as a thing of humour?'

The English language contains different lengths of vowel sounds. For example, it will take you slightly longer to say the diphthong 'I' than it does to say the short 'i' in 'it'. Check that you don't reduce all vowels to short vowels. Consonants must be used firmly. If you have to say a word like 'ghosts', you must work your way right through the 's', then 't', then 's' because anything else will be unclear to your listeners. They will spend precious seconds trying to sort out by context what you've said and therefore miss your next point.

EXERCISE

Tape yourself and listen to your voice. Practise tongue twisters or repetition phrases, such as 'Unique New York, New York's unique' or 'Red leather, yellow leather, red leather, yellow leather'.

Intonation

Variation of pitch adds life and colour to your voice. Think in terms of highs and lows or allowing the voice to rise and fall naturally. It doesn't take very much alteration of pitch to make your voice interesting. Usually you alter pitch for emphasis and you should do this on only the main syllable of a word. For example, with 'Oh, that's interesting', you could pitch up on the 'in' of interesting. Or you could pitch up on 'that's' and you would get a slightly different meaning. Try it!

EXERCISE

- Read stories to children (or to anyone else kind enough to listen). Experiment with highs and lows, injecting passion into your voice.
- Sing the 'Do-Re-Mi' scales.

Inflections

In some parts of the world, people raise the pitch of their voice at the end of a sentence, thereby turning it into a question. This can be confusing for the listener. Often this rising inflection can be attributed to a soft palate (located at the back of the roof of the mouth), which is lowering instead of lifting. It is very difficult both to articulate and to use a wide pitch range when the soft palate is lowered.

EXERCISE

Get into the habit of making statements. Think 'down' at the ends of sentences, and don't turn the sentence into a question. Get feedback as to whether or not you do this.

Avoiding falsetto pitch

Many women speak in a pitch that is unnaturally high. They are often using 'falsetto quality' instead of 'speech quality'. In speech quality the vocal folds are short and thick, producing a different tone quality from falsetto, where the vocal folds are thin and stiff. Try to achieve glottal onset of tone, which means the vocal folds come together the instant before speech starts — try using the cheeky 'uh oh' sounds we make when we see trouble looming. This usually places us in speech quality.

A characteristic of falsetto quality is that the breath escapes just before the tone starts, and using the vowel sounds in the exercises below will also ensure that this doesn't happen.

EXERCISE

A good way to avoid falsetto voice pitch is to practise lots of sentences where each word begins with a vowel. 'Angry ants activate acid' or 'Elegant elephants eat everything' are good examples.

Another idea is to count backwards from five, lowering the pitch slightly each time. By the time you get to 'two' or 'one', you've probably hit the pitch which is more naturally your own, instead of the one you habitually use.

Volume

Your volume depends on the size of the room. If you are speaking in a small room, use your natural voice. If in a larger room, project to the last row. If you can't be heard, all your key messages are lost. Never push from the larynx to get louder. Rather, use the muscles of the back to ensure that you achieve more volume by trying the exercise below.

EXERCISE

Imagine you have a balloon under each armpit and that you are squashing them against your sides as you speak without the audience seeing any effort on your part. Next, find what movement creates a 'fat waist', where your waist muscles on either side seem to push out a little. It's what happens naturally when you actively hold your breath. A little engagement of these muscles on either side of the spine will increase your volume by 10–15 decibels without putting stress on your larynx.

Get someone to stand at the back of the room when you are

rehearsing your speech and let you know you if you are projecting your voice sufficiently.

Pace

Speed means the number of words spoken per minute. Most of us speak at a rate of about 160–200 words per minute. In December 1961, John F. Kennedy gave a speech at the rate of 327 words per minute — I hope the audience could understand it!

Move quickly through the unimportant words and phrases and slow down the important ones. It is this variety of pace which makes us sound interesting. A constant pace, either fast or slow, is difficult to stay tuned in to; it becomes mesmeric.

EXERCISE

Listen to other speakers and become conscious of their pace. When do they speed up? When do they slow down? Listening to others will improve your skill.

Pauses

Actors use a pause to create suspense and gain the audience's attention. Pausing is more effective than using fillers like 'um' and 'ah'. Silence is powerful. Listeners tend to hang on in anticipation of a speaker choosing exactly the word they need to describe something accurately. Never forget that we are fascinated by the spectacle of someone in the act of thinking.

> *'The most precious thing in speeches are the pauses.'*
> — Sir Ralph Richardson, actor

EXERCISE

Pause and inhale every time you go to say 'um' or 'ah' or use a filler word. Ask friends and colleagues if you use 'ums' and 'ahs' in your conversations. Video yourself giving a 2-minute speech and work towards not saying 'um' any more than once a minute.

Build to a pause by making three specific points, each one slightly higher in pitch than the one before. By the time you've done that, you've earned yourself a pause, while the listeners digest the information you've given them and you let the words 'hang in the air' for a short space of time. The three-point plan seems to be particularly satisfying for human beings to listen and relate to. You can often 'cap' these points with a summing-up sentence in a lower pitch.

Overcoming stuttering

It takes patience, skill and professional support to overcome a stutter. Winston Churchill had a stutter when he started his career. Through sheer determination and effort he became one of the most accomplished orators of the twentieth century.

I have worked with a number of clients who stutter when they are nervous, especially when having to speak on television. They include a chief executive who was terrified he would stutter if stuck for words. The more he relaxed his voice and practised vocal warm-up exercises like humming and relaxing the body, the less he stuttered.

Another businessman came for coaching after a stuttering episode on national television. I felt so sorry for him when I saw the footage and his level of discomfort. It was a news item and he panicked when confronted with a challenging question. He stuttered over and over. Fear does extraordinary things to the body and voice.

If you are a chronic stutterer I strongly encourage you to get a voice coach or seek other professional help to overcome your fears. There is often an emotional or psychological issue behind the stutter.

EXERCISE

Try allowing an easy, full breath in and then chant what you want to say. Chanting requires an even flow of breath and means that you must work at a slowish pace in order to articulate all the sounds in the words. From there, it is relatively easy to release the chant (which is halfway between speech and singing) back to ordinary speech.

Microphones

Practise and make sure you feel comfortable with a microphone. There are many different varieties so check in advance what will be available on the day of your presentation and don't make assumptions. I've seen many speakers turn up to speak who have never used one before. Microphones enable you to speak more easily in a large room and not strain your voice. During a Skype presentation make sure the sound is turned up, that you're projecting your voice, and that all parties hear you. I've seen technology break down on many occasions and people get frustrated. Have a back-up plan.

Make sure you turn off your microphone when you are no longer presenting lest you do the same as a television newsreader who forgot to turn off her microphone when going to the bathroom. An embarrassing mistake!

Chapter 12 on technology has a list of tips for using your microphone effectively.

EXERCISE

Do a sound check at least an hour before your presentation. If you've never used a microphone before, practise with it so it's not foreign to you. Never get up on a platform or rostrum and say, 'Is this microphone on? Can you hear me?' You will look unprepared and it's a flat way to open your speech.

If you want to practise at home with a microphone, many sound systems have a karaoke function that allows you to listen to yourself speaking.

Looking after your voice

A friend who is a member of parliament was telling me that his voice gets very tired at the end of the day when he is on the campaign trail. As most of you know, an MP will present on a street corner, in a church hall, door knocking, on a stage, in one-on-one conversations, shops — anywhere and everywhere from dawn to dusk. Here are some tips I gave him.

- Rest your voice when you get home for as long as you can. Try to keep off the phone for at least eight hours, which should be your sleeping time. The best solution is to stop talking.
- Laughing relaxes the vocal cords by allowing them to vibrate without hindrance, which is what happens when a speaker

'opens the throat'. Ellen Sarewitz said, 'When I become tense and the sound is strained, my singing teacher makes me laugh, which immediately removes the stress and allows the notes to go into the right place.'

- Keep hydrated. If your throat is sore, drink water at room temperature.
- Keep right away from cigarettes. They'll not only ruin your voice, they'll eventually kill you. If you're reading this chapter and you are a smoker, sorry to offend, but it might pay to do some research on the damage it does to your voice.

Taking care of your voice is really important. Voice teacher Linda Cartwright teaches her students how to look after their vocal folds. The diagram below shows a view of the larynx — note the false folds situated just above the true folds. They can come together to close up the airspace above the true vocal folds and this upsets vibration and the sound quality of your voice. I know this sounds very technical but it is worthwhile researching the voice apparatus, especially if you're presenting often.

LARYNX

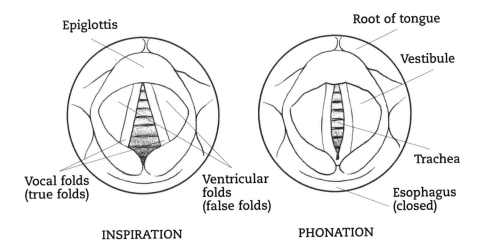

TIPS ON A BETTER VOICE

(by Linda Cartwright, voice teacher)

- Take care of your voice and don't take it for granted. This includes avoiding smoke-filled rooms, pushing out volume without supporting the larynx and thrusting your chin forward when speaking.

- Stand with a lengthened spine and relax any muscles that aren't actively involved in holding your body up.

- Drive the energy through from the beginning of a sentence to the end of the sentence. This avoids a 'dropping off' rhythm, which becomes irritating to listeners.

- Speak clearly and repeat diction exercises to exercise the tongue muscles.

- Flow phrases on so that you are shaping the words into a form that is easily understood by your listeners. We hear in phrases, not in a series of individual words. Often, in order to try to achieve clarity, people will speak giving each word the same value. This will simply sound pedantic and monotonous.

- Vary your pitch and pace. We often interrupt ourselves, remember an example, or bring in a new idea when we're speaking. Each time we do this, we bring a renewed energy to our voices. We speak a little faster, and we slightly alter our pitch. Check that you're doing this. It will give the appearance of spontaneity and keep the listeners' attention.

5
First Impressions

'It's not the impression you make,
it's the impression you leave.'

— Tennessee woman remembering Marilyn Schwartz,
her old Southern grandmother

As author John Malloy says, 'You don't get a second chance to make a first impression.' Whether you appear on television, present online, run your first team meeting or front up on day one at a new job, a good first impression always gets you off to a good start.

While it used to be that you had 30 seconds to make a first impression, research shows that the time is now much shorter. In fact, we're all making judgments within 'the blink of an eye'! A series of experiments by Princeton psychologists Janine Willis and Alexander Todorov show it only takes a tenth of a second to form an impression of a stranger from their face, and that longer exposures don't significantly alter those impressions (although they might boost your confidence in your judgments).

The audience decides whether or not to trust you based on their first impressions. The way I see it is that we're all tuned in to our favourite radio station: WIIFM (What's in it for me?). When we meet someone for the first time, we always think, 'Do I like you? What's in it for me to be in a relationship with you?'

Harvard Business School Social psychologist Amy Cuddy studies how we evaluate people. She says when we form first impressions of other people we actually form two impressions. We judge how warm and trustworthy the person is so we can decide what their intentions are towards us and we also ask how strong and competent they are, assessing whether they're capable of enacting their intentions. Research shows these two traits account for 80 to 90 per cent of overall first impressions across all cultures.

In my work I encounter first impressions every time I coach someone or run a course. However, my first impressions start well before I meet the client or run the first exercise. They start with the first phone call, email or their pre-course questionnaire and continue when they arrive in the classroom or get out of the lift. I notice warmth, reluctance or fear. I notice eye contact, handshakes, demeanour and dress. What's interesting is that sometimes these impressions differ from the first impression I get when the same people do their first impromptu exercise. They stop gesturing, stop smiling and step into what they think is an appropriate persona for public performance.

Pay attention to bad habits and distractions that can immediately cre-

ate a bad impression you don't need or deserve. These are things like chewing gum, not smiling, a feeble or over-zealous handshake, lack of eye contact, mumbling your name, or engaging with distractions like iPhones that are inappropriate for the occasion. Go into meetings, appointments, courses and events determined to focus 100 per cent of your concentration and energy on the job in hand.

Your opening is critical

If you are presenting or making a speech your opening is critical. Take your position on the stage with confidence and poise. Walk purposefully, smile, keep your eyes up, stop when you get to the lectern or speaking space, pause, breathe, look at your audience warmly and then start speaking.

This is a performance! You need to get their attention, get them on your side and get them interested in what you've got to say from the get go. If you haven't presented before it's essential to rehearse openings several times so they can be delivered with confidence and presence. Even if you're nervous, 'fake it until you make it', create the impression you're pleased to be there and have something to say. The audience won't want to listen to a grumpy speaker who comes across as a 'cold fish'.

Sometimes the very first impression I get from someone can be grumpy and it takes time for this to change. For example, Janet is a highly respected manager who walked in to one of my workshops with a frown on her face that lasted for at least 15 minutes. I was concerned because she was very cold and I wasn't sure if she was upset or angry about participating. After I'd heard her talk about her fear of public speaking, four hours later, I realized she was simply nervous. As she left the programme she said it had taken her completely out of her comfort zone.

Ali is a receptionist at a hotel I stay in frequently. When I first met him, he gave me almost no eye contact, and looked grumpy and totally disengaged. This annoyed me so much I decided to see what happened if I over-engaged and responded with some of the behaviour I would've liked from him. So, I gave him full-on eye contact, called him by his name and said, 'Hello Ali, it's great to be here. How's your day been? Have you been enjoying your work today?' Suddenly he started to thaw and the inkling of a smile emerged. This gave me an opening to keep the conversation going and enlist him in quite a different way. Now he's a new man; he beams at my colleagues and me, asks how I am and is attentive beyond belief! There are lots of Alis around — people who are by-passed, overlooked and maybe not enjoying their work. They don't realize that what they put out is what they get back. Sometimes we have a purpose to cheer them up and turn them around!

What first impression do you make?

Ask three people you respect what their first impressions were when they met you. Record their answers. If they're all favourable keep asking until you get constructive negative criticism. Ask them to be specific. For example, if you came across as cold, arrogant or cynical, was it in your eyes, body language or tone of voice? Keep on asking, record it and listen without being defensive. If someone has told you your shoes are not polished, or your tie is worn, take it onboard — clean your shoes and buy a new tie! Don't waste time judging or beating up on yourself; do something positive with the information.

Amelia is an American living in the United Kingdom. Her team was pitching for a large piece of business to a significant audience in a public relations company in London. While Amelia and her two colleagues arrived on time, the group managing director of her company misjudged things, arrived an hour late and then spent 10 minutes apologizing. At that moment, Amelia knew they had lost the pitch before they'd even started. 'I was furious and very disappointed because we should have won it,' she said.

Always focus on the end goal. Arrive early, leave yourself enough time and assume nothing. This error of judgment not only lost the company a job, but the manager let down his team and his behaviour damaged the company's reputation. If you are late for a meeting you send a message that says, 'It's not important enough.' Creating a good first impression is about respecting others and making sure that things like this don't happen. It probably took this manager several months to restore his reputation with his team and a significant PR audience. Don't self-sabotage!

Your friends make an impression on you

Blessed with a close group of friends, I often think of the first time I met them individually. All these people I love and confide in have had a huge impact on my life. I can remember the first time I met every one of them. Take your mind back to when you met your close friends and clients. Why were you drawn to them? Was it their appearance, energy, cheekiness, personality, intelligence, spark, authenticity, beauty or overall humanity? These people were all strangers at one time, but through conversations, dinners, exchanges of ideas and information, they have become friends. Every one of them made a first impression that stayed with you and led to a lasting friendship. I worked on a television show many years ago in New Zealand and clicked with one woman, in particular, who was very striking, interesting to talk to and strong. We had so many things in common and similar values and we felt like we'd been friends forever. Today we are lifelong friends.

How to make a good first impression

You need to engage your audience warmly and authentically in the first 30 seconds and that's all about the 'P' words: preparation, presence, projection, pizzazz and practice.

Here are some things to think about.

Planning

Making an impression requires making an effort. Know your opening, your key messages and your stories inside out. Think carefully about your audience and consider how you can connect with them. Who are they? Are they a professional or business audience, a community group, colleagues, old, young, racially mixed or a specific culture? Are they well informed about the topic, or do they know nothing about it? Are they likely to be hostile, supportive, passive or active? What do they have in common and what do you have in common with them?

Why have they come to listen to you? Perhaps they want to, maybe they've been told to or maybe they share your politics or cause. Do they want to learn, be amused or entertained or are they 'ticking the boxes' as part of their professional development?

Your objective

Define your objective. Is it to bring in more business or attract new clients? Is it to raise money for a cause you believe in, talk about leadership or launch a new project? In the end your job is to move, touch and inspire people, so a great opening is essential if you want to do that.

Add value

If you have an opportunity, dress the set to help you enhance your story. Maybe a photo slide show or some music would add real value? What about your company banner or a pull-up sign? Think about great props that reinforce your message or even a series of hats.

Image

How do you want to be perceived? The clothing you wear tells people a lot about who you are. Invest in your image. If this is not your strong suit it's not overly expensive to hire an image consultant. Some stores, especially those that know you will give you this service for free. Talk to a friend who has flair with clothes and accessories. Spend an afternoon going through your wardrobe with that person and think about some new, more interesting ways to put your existing clothes together. (See Chapter 15.)

Voice

Work with a coach or a professional actor and learn how to use your voice to your best advantage. Or ask someone to film your performance, then critique your voice and work on it yourself. (See Chapter 4.)

Workshop your opening lines

You'll need to introduce yourself if someone else doesn't do it. Welcome the audience, thank them for coming and find a powerful and memorable way to get into your topic. Always allow time to acknowledge other speakers and significant people in the audience. (See Chapter 10.)

Leave-behind documents

Have a great business card and always carry it with you. Keep some on hand to give to people you meet before or after the presentation and leave some at the back of the venue — always make sure they're clean.

Get your 'leave-behind' document copied and make it available with your card. Make sure it is copyrighted, attractively branded and professional. If you have books, CDs or DVDs of your work available put these out on display too.

Promotion

Marketing is essential when wanting to make a strong impression. Hire a public relations consultant to make you look good or find a mentor where there is no cost. You can hire a publicist for a one-off project and that could be something as small as getting you an article in a women's magazine.

Passion

Speak from the heart and people will be motivated to listen. Show others you're willing to share your feelings and opinions with emotion. Move your audience to listen and want more. It's perfectly OK to show you care by wearing your heart on your sleeve.

Encourage participation

Make some of your presentation interactive. People pay more attention when they feel included. Communication is a two-way exchange.

Self-promotion

Antipodeans don't brag enough. Our culture of understatement and laconic expression encourages us to undersell ourselves, even when we've excelled internationally or won Olympic gold. One of the things I loved about living in America was that it is acceptable to talk proudly about your skills. Don't be afraid to promote yourself, but do it with sincerity and integrity. Remember that your accomplishments are facts, not a sign of arrogance. I'm often amazed to discover the extraordinary things clients have done, but extracting this information can be like pulling teeth. Share who you really are — people want to meet the real you.

> 'Your appearance can raise expectations, but what you saw and how you say it will determine how people evaluate you.' — Carroll O'Connor, film and television actor

Your working environment

Project the image you want others to have of you. If you want to be perceived as professional, then make an effort to be tidy and present your office well. Don't be afraid to show your personality in your office or your noticeboard if this is appropriate where you work. Personal photos are a handy icebreaker. Think about fresh flowers or great pot plants to cheer yourself and others up.

Résumés

Your résumé will get you the job interview, so remember this is your first chance to make an impression before you do so in person. Make sure your résumé is professional, reflects your values, skills and achievements, and is kept up to date and well designed. It needs to sell you, but it shouldn't over-sell in a way that is not credible. Pay attention to coherence, facts and accuracy. Provide context and consider using short attributions to substantiate your achievements. If you have a number of 'different strings to your bow', take time to develop a couple of different versions and always have a variety of summary profiles on hand that you can use to promote yourself.

Get hold of three excellent curricula vitae that have helped other people get jobs and look at what they've done. Work on yours then show it to friends, colleagues or mentors and ask for feedback; they will probably notice things that you might have missed. Would you hire yourself based on your CV?

Other written communication

For many people, email is an important communication tool. However, we often present ourselves poorly via this medium.

An email reflects your personality, your company brand and your attitude. Read what you've written carefully, make sure the tone and manner is warm and professional, that the words say what you want them to say and answer the questions that have been asked. Cut-to-the-chase, edit, edit, edit and make it easy for the recipient to receive and comprehend.

If you're motivated to send an angry email or text, think about how you want to be perceived before you press the send button. Consider saving it, cooling down and reflecting on it again.

Spell check and proofread your message carefully.

Be very careful about sending confidential information in a business or public service environment. Many people end up in disastrous situations because they are simply too casual and forget that emails provide a written record of their personal and professional behaviour, can be recovered forensically and in some circumstances requested under legal instructions or directions.

Job interviews

Thirty per cent of my work is about helping clients prepare for and win either contracts or the job of their dreams. Their success is my success.

I always pay attention to feedback and often ask for it directly. Not knowing what impression you've made can leave you wondering.

Brian is a triple A graduate and couldn't understand why he wasn't getting the job. His family invested in a training package and we met weekly over many weeks, filming interviews as he started to come out of his shell. He realized he was not coming across confidently in interviews. He wasn't smiling, he wasn't projecting his voice, and wasn't comfortable answering standard questions that anyone would be asked in a job interview. Brian is now doing well in the job of his dreams. His mother still talks about the changes she saw after the regular training sessions.

I was having a conversation with a general manager who interviewed a woman for a senior human resources position. The chief executive was present at the interview also. The general manager wanted to hire her because she had all the credentials and she thought she looked great, funky and high fashion. The CEO didn't agree and the next day she asked him why he didn't hire her. His reply? 'I didn't like her clothes.' The man who got the job wore very conservative suits. The moral of the story is you could be the perfect candidate for the job but for whatever reason your first impression hasn't spoken to the decision-maker. Don't take it personally.

I always encourage my clients to meet with me and decide whether or not they want to work with me. In reality they are interviewing me. Remember, interviews are a two-way process. I was in email contact with a potential client before meeting face to face. I asked her to be very open in her brief to me. When I finally walked in to the café to meet her I saw her smiling face and she radiated warmth. Instead of shaking hands, which I would normally do, we gave each other a big hug. This is not my normal practice in a business meeting but she was open, friendly and warm. It just felt like a natural thing to do. This was the start of a good business relationship. Not only do you make a first impression in person but also over email.

A checklist for job interviews

1. Do your research. Know what the organization you're applying to does, what they're famous for, who their clients are, what their culture is like and the type of people they employ.

2. If possible, find out who's going to be on the interview panel, what interests they will represent and how it will be structured.

3. Be prepared from the outset. Rehearse your questions before you turn up. Plan to answer softer personal questions as well as hard ones. Think about examples you can provide in advance.

4. Know your strengths and weaknesses. Be able to describe clearly, and in a few punchy points, how your personal skills and attributes can add value.

5. Wear appropriate clothing. Less is definitely more when it comes to how you dress. Keep it simple, clean and uncluttered. You want the focus to be on you, not your glitzy earrings or polka-dotted bowtie.

6. Know where you are going and leave plenty of time to get there. Being late won't help your stress levels!

7. Ask questions. You are not only the interviewee but also an interviewer, so think carefully about the things you want to know and ask questions that will help you understand the job more fully.

8. Show respect and be polite.

9. Read between the lines. Even though you'll often never really know what the interviewers thought of you, ask for feedback if you don't progress through the process or get the job.

10. Never give up. Pursue your dream regardless of the knockbacks. Don't take rejection personally; it's tough looking for jobs and the market is becoming increasingly competitive. Learn from the experience and polish your performance for next time.

11. Finally, always be true to yourself.

Networking

Networking is essential in business and being confident allows you to make a good first impression. Networking with confidence will help your career and help you grow as a person. Making small talk at functions is a frightening experience for many people. Rather than thinking of it as schmoozing, think of it as networking, making new friends and having interesting conversations.

I've designed programmes for years on networking and changed them according to clients' needs. I'm constantly amazed at the number of people who tell me that they do not feel comfortable or confident walking into a room of strangers. We have a networking programme that teaches people how to work a room, start up new conversations, exit and move on. How do you get past 'hello'? My advice is be yourself, be present when talking to people and listen. When you meet someone for the first time, focus on what they are saying not on what you want to say. Take the focus off yourself by thinking about the other person. If you want people to spend time with you, being authentic is all that really matters. If you find your eyes drifting off at a function, come back. It sends out a single that you're not interested. This makes a bad first impression.

Turn up to functions to grow your network of clients and friends. Face-to-face conversations are always a more powerful way to connect with others and present yourself. You never know what you're going to walk away with. The number one rule is to always take plenty of business cards and contact the person the following day just to say it was a pleasure to meet with them and to set up a coffee meeting. That new contact is just sitting there waiting for you. I've never yet walked away from a networking function without a new business contact.

Listening

The golden rule is to avoid talking about yourself all the time. I see many people asking questions at business and private functions but not listening to the answers. Make the other person feel important by asking questions and listening to their answers. It will show in your eyes if you're not attentive. The whole point of networking is to expand your professional relationships; the key to any good relationship is to listen in such a way that people remember you. We use theatre exercises with our clients working in pairs to demonstrate this.

Your appearance

See Chapter 15 for tips on brushing up your wardrobe and presenting yourself well.

TIPS ON MAKING A GOOD FIRST IMPRESSION

- Plan your wardrobe in advance of an important speech, interview or meeting. Wear clothing that makes you feel comfortable.

- Take pride in your appearance — polished shoes and a manicure speak volumes.

- Check your personal hygiene: bad breath, body odour and an unshaven face all send a strong message of not caring about yourself.

- Avoid overpowering perfume or cologne.

- Have a firm handshake. Carrying your briefcase or your handbag in your left hand allows you to shake hands with your right.

- Smile and radiate warmth when you meet someone for the first time.

- Eye contact is important.

- Good posture tells us that you're confident. Shoulders back and hold the head up straight.

- Bring energy to every conversation, even if you are exhausted.

- Ask questions and be genuinely interested when hearing the answer. People love to be listened to. Practise being a good listener.

- Have a positive attitude.

6
Developing and Writing Content

'The main thing is to keep the main thing the main thing.'

— Dr Stephen Covey, author, teacher and leadership coach

Competing with noise

In today's digital age of global communication, competition for our attention is intense and increasing by the second — so great words and content matter.

Whether via our eyeballs, our ears, our mind, our heart, our friends, families or networks, people are trying to entertain us, influence us, sell us something, change us, enrol us, inform us or improve us.

Surrounding this is an overwhelming soundscape of babble, chatter and opinions as millions of Facebook posts and tweets travel the world and vie for our attention on a daily basis. A landslide of uploaded videos, photographs, graphics, statistics and data also competes for our time, while marketers and advertisers work sophisticated magic collecting 'big data' to target our interests and send us more.

You're overwhelmed with this! So am I!

Trying to write a meaningful speech or even a competent presentation in an increasingly digital world is a frequently daunting task. What keeps me sane is trying to simplify stories for others. Keeping it simple and going back to the beginning always helps. Once I've got that bit together I can usually follow some of my own advice and write the speech or plan the presentation. That's the theory anyway.

Over the years I've listened to hundreds of presentations and speeches in different countries, and in different contexts, from simple and personal to more complex and corporate. In the end I always come back to this basic question: 'How can I move, inspire and engage my audience?'

Here's our Fresh Eyre ten-point plan

1. Do your homework.
2. Focus on what you want to say (the one thing).
3. Support it with two or three supporting messages.
4. Cut the jargon — write it to speak it.
5. Bring it to life with stories, anecdotes and examples.
6. Provide context and back yourself with great statistics.
7. Develop a coherent structure and stick to it.
8. Hook your audience with a powerful introduction.
9. Tie it all up with a strong ending.
10. Review, read it aloud (constantly) and edit, edit, edit.

Above all be authentic, passionate and memorable!

> '*The best way to sound like you know what you're talking about is to know what you're talking about.*'
> — Unknown

Doing your homework

The key to writing a memorable speech is preparation. If you give yourself enough time to prepare properly without pressure, you'll be able to sort out any problems and make sure you're saying what you really want to say.

What's the job at hand? What do you want/need to say to your team, your staff, your business, your local community, your shareholders, suppliers, clients, stakeholders, constituents?

If it's more personal, what do you want/need to say at a family gathering, funeral, wedding or celebration you're leading for friends? Alternatively, what have you been asked to talk about?

Why you?

- Are you a local/national or industry expert on the issue?
- Are you a 'storyteller to die for'?
- Do you have a point of view that needs to be represented?
- Are you the 'architect' of a new scheme or programme?
- Does 'the buck stop with you'?
- Are you the 'star turn' for the evening?
- Are you the inspirational speaker for a conference?

What's the context?

The more you can find out about the event you're speaking at or presenting in the better.

- Why is it being held? What do you or the organizers want from it?
- Is it an opening or closing speech? If so what else is likely to happen; that is, cutting a ribbon, unveiling a plaque or taking the cork off a bottle of champagne?
- How big will it be?
- Who will be in the audience?
- Where will you fit in the pecking order; that is, are you the first or last speaker or somewhere in between?
- Who are the other speakers and what have they been asked to talk about?
- Will formal acknowledgements/introductions be needed? If so, who can provide you with their formal titles and the correct pecking order?
- How long should your speech be? Find out the time and stick to it.

- Will there be time for questions and how will this be managed; that is, written questions in advance or questions from the floor?
- How will your speech/presentation fit in to the event? Are you providing opening remarks as the MC? Are you a keynote speaker, part of a workshop or on a panel?
- What's the dress code (casual, semi-formal, formal, military, academic)?
- Are there difficulties/problems you should know about in advance?
- Is there an advance deadline for you to send your presentation to the organizers? If so, when? And who should you send it to?
- Do you need to write a synopsis or send a biography and a photograph for forward publicity?
- What leave-behind documents are required?

Content

Once you have the context for the speech, know and understand what's required, you can start thinking about your content.

Being original is all-important. I have heard the same speech given by a high-profile personality at two different black-tie dinners. The only conversation at my table was how every guest had heard it before. This is not good for your reputation.

If the speech is about your life story you'll obviously know the content; however, you may need help to make it interesting. Here are some questions to ask yourself to get started.

- What motivates, excites or delights you?
- What is the one thing you're most proud of?
- What is the biggest mistake you've made and how have you learnt from it?
- What is the worst moment in your life and how did you come back from it?
- What are the three lessons you've learnt in life?

- Who are the three people who've helped you along the way?
- Think about your family and their influence on you.
- Think about school and other educational influences.
- Who are your heroes?
- What is the one thing that's got you through or helped you succeed?
- What would you most like to be remembered for?

Business presentations and speeches

If you're developing content for a business presentation, consider the questions listed above and see if you can use or adapt them for your speech. Connecting with your audience is vital; people are more likely to listen to you and learn from you if they see you as a person they can relate to.

Now step aside from your work and think about all these things you may have in common with your audience. Do you:

- Share the same workplace?
- Work in the same industry or used to?
- Live in the same town or used to?
- Work in a different industry but share things in common?
- Have the same problems (hearing, wearing glasses, smoking, over-eating, heart disease, cancer, money worries)?
- Share the same interests/enthusiasms (animals, history, sport, music)?
- Share the same age, ethnicity or sex?
- Have or are a parent/have elderly parents?
- Have a similar experience (weather, an earthquake, electricity blackouts, petrol rises, a bus strike, traffic congestion)?

NOTE: *You may not find out all these things before you write your speech, but you can observe the audience before you speak. You may even talk to people in a prior tea break to get some spontaneous ideas.*

This list may also prompt ideas for questions, comments or icebreakers.

Ask more questions

Talk to your kids, your colleagues, an expert in the field — anyone who can provide insight into what you're talking about; anyone who can help you focus on what would make it useful and interesting to the audience.

Online research

I always start by going to the group's website. Look at their history, their claim to fame. Who's who 'in their zoo'? Have they won an award or a competition, built a new building, started a new initiative, raised money for charity or been in the media? Do they have a motto and, if so, does it connect with your vision? Is this something you could talk about? It's always worth checking out their vision and mission statements, looking at their online news, and checking out what other people say about them.

Presenting to your colleagues

Never take a business presentation to your team or colleagues for granted. They're probably your most important audience. They need to understand the big picture, where the organization is heading, what its goals and challenges are, and how you want them to deliver your organizational strategy. They're the people who will communicate key strategies and messages to staff across the organization, so if they don't 'get' what needs to be 'got' nobody else will.

Here are some Fresh Eyre basics

- Be energetic, lively and engaging.
- Be reliable, keep to time and stick to the agenda you've set.
- Be prepared, circulate important documents in advance and bring hard copies if needed. Share contextual information, useful 'intelligence' and helpful summaries.
- Outline what you plan to do, do it and summarize key action points at the end.
- Don't bore people with complex/jargon-ridden language or tedious PowerPoint presentations.

- Follow the ABC (accuracy, brevity and clarity).
- Inject humour into your presentation.
- Think about how you can be memorable.
- Tell stories and give examples.
- Show you're willing to listen, and answer questions.
- Learn how to 'park' distractions and deal with them respectfully later.

Developing structure

Keep it simple. A good speech needs to have a great introduction and a powerful, memorable ending. Sometimes it's useful to design a writing template and work through it. This takes the pressure off writing the intro first. Below is one that you can adapt. We've tried this with hundreds of different groups, from refugees and migrants to high-performance athletes and rural service advisors.

Introduction

Greetings: Good Evening/Good morning/or a greeting in your native language, etc.

I'm ... : (Give your first name and surname, say them slowly and proudly)

I come from:

I'm from/I am or both: (Insert your/home country/town/ occupation and your claim to fame.) For example, 'I come from Christchurch, I'm a rally car driver, currently competing in the World Rally Championship — after five rounds we're now sitting sixth in the championship.'

Thank you for the opportunity to come and talk to you today.

Thank you to: (If appropriate your key sponsors/the conference organizers/groups who have provided entertainment.)

Other acknowledgements: (If appropriate: significant leaders/ public dignitaries other teams/your competitors/your family.)

Today I want to talk to you about: (How I got into motor sport/high-performance rowing/how I came here as a refugee/why I love being a nurse.)

Start at the beginning: (Talk about what got you into motor sport/rowing/nursing/what brought you here as a refugee/or whatever is relevant to your audience.)

Think of an appropriate story and note it: (For example, 'A story about winning at the world championships' or 'leaving Sudan' or 'working in the rest home'.)

Inspiration: (People who helped you get where you are today. We suggest you name about three, for example, your parents or a family member, a coach/mentor or sponsor, a teacher/friend or colleague.)

The influence of school: (Omit if not helpful or appropriate.)

Three things I've learnt along the way: (Name each and say why it's been important to you; for example, patience, hard work and generosity.)

The most important thing: (This is an opportunity to finish strongly; for example, 'In the end I've only got where I am today through the generosity of others.')

Thank you very much.

This speech can be really powerful and usually runs for 5 to 10 minutes. Think of your own ways to 'add value' by using photos, maps and props. The key is to be authentic, keep it real, inject stories and anecdotes to bring it to life, and practise, practise, practise.

Key messages

Your key message is the one thing you want to say or convey to your audience. Start by summarizing it into a short paragraph and then reduce it to one strong, clear, memorable sentence. Essentially, this is the coathanger on which the rest of your speech will hang. It's the theme you'll come back to during your speech.

Components of a good key message include:

- Cutting to the chase.
- Saying what you mean and meaning what you say.
- Using strong visual language; in other words, paint pictures verbally.
- Being memorable.
- Techniques like metaphor, simile and alliteration can all be powerful.
- Using strong statistics and humanizing them.
- Remembering the ABC — accuracy, brevity and clarity.

Example

This speech on misogyny was delivered by former Australian Prime Minister Julia Gillard on 9 October 2012 in reaction to alleged sexism from opposition leader Tony Abbott. It is a fascinating example of a speech that received great international coverage but a more mixed reaction 'at home'. This is a very strong, brave speech that uses repetition well. Note how well she 'nails' the strong statement in the first message with subsequent messages. Within a week, a YouTube version of the speech had had 1 million views. (Link: https://www.youtube.com/watch?v=SOPsxp-MzYw4) By 2014 the ABC news video had had 2.6 million views.

The key message of the speech was this: 'I will not be lectured about sexism and misogyny by this man. I will not. And the government will not be lectured about sexism and misogyny by this man. Not now, not ever.'

The supporting messages of this speech included:

- 'The Leader of the Opposition says that people who hold sexist views and who are misogynists are not appropriate for high office. Well, I hope the Leader of the Opposition has got a piece of paper and is writing out his resignation. Because if he wants to know what misogyny looks like in modern Australia, he doesn't need a motion in the House of Representatives, he needs a mirror.'

- 'I was very offended personally when the Leader of the Opposition, as Minister of Health, said, and I quote, "Abortion is the easy way out." '
- 'I was also very offended on behalf of the women of Australia when in the course of this carbon pricing campaign, the Leader of the Opposition said, "What the housewives of Australia need to understand as they do the ironing ..." Thank you for that painting of women's roles in modern Australia.'
- 'I was offended too by the sexism, by the misogyny of the Leader of the Opposition catcalling across this table at me as I sit here as Prime Minister.'

Openings and introductions

Ask yourself this question every time. 'What response do I want in the first 30 seconds?' Think back to all the speeches you've listened to and who made the most impact and why.

Grab your audience's attention right from the start. Give your audience a reason for listening and being in the room.

Here are some examples we've created to show you how memorable language, imagery, juxtaposition of ideas, and smart use of language can make for a good introduction.

Example 1

My friends tell me I'm half the man I used to be. Today I feel larger than life! Ladies and gentlemen, tonight I want to share the story of how I've halved my size in the past two years and won my own battle with obesity.

Example 2

Picture this: 100 years ago Kapiti Island was a barren wilderness, grazed by a few marauding sheep and overrun by rats. Today it is dense with native forest, and teaming with native birds — many of them endangered species. This morning I want to tell you the remarkable story of how Kapiti Island became New Zealand's first international bird sanctuary.

Example 3

Six years ago, I was diagnosed HIV positive. It was the first time I'd been positive about anything in my life. My name is John Smith [not his real name] and today I want to tell you about how the worst news I ever received was the best thing that ever happened to me.

What makes things memorable?

Show me, don't tell me

My colleague Allie Webber recalls advice given to her as a young documentary filmmaker: 'The film-making mantra I grew up with still holds good today and it's great advice for speech writing. It's the concept of "show me don't tell me". In summary, take me somewhere I've never been before, introduce me to someone I've never met before, and help me to think of things in a new or different way.'

Tell stories

> 'People are more impressed by the power of our example rather than the example of our power ...'
> — Bill Clinton, former US president

Stories are gold and are nearly always the most memorable part of a speech. One of the things that makes coaching and training so special for me is the stories people tell me about their lives; the before and after stories, stories of generosity, compassion, kindness, growing confidence and leadership.

These are the 'take-home' bits we recount to our friends and families 'after the show'. Learn to listen to them, collect them, edit them, polish them up, save them and inject them into your speeches and presentations at every opportunity. Be confident telling them, use your own language and bring them to life. Design them to be roughly 2 minutes each and then practise by editing them down to powerful 1-minute and 30-second versions.

If you're in a more managerial or supervisory position and not out and about seeing and hearing things for yourself, get your colleagues and staff to pass on stories, anecdotes and comments to you.

These are some of the techniques you can use to put them into your speeches.

- 'Only last week, one of our supervisors told me a brilliant story about how our new disability aids have changed the lives of one family ...'
- 'For reasons of confidentiality I can't give names but in general these are the kinds of things we hear ...'
- 'I've changed the names but here are three case histories that demonstrate how positive this scheme has been ...'

The magic seven

Accelerated learning techniques show that most people can't remember more than seven words or digits without applying other techniques to help them. Hence many phone numbers in the world are only seven digits. We remember longer numbers by 'chunking' or breaking it up. We remember the international codes and the area codes and put them first, then we break the number down into blocks of three or four, so I remember my phone number in three blocks of three for example.

Think about the poems, hymns or quotes you learnt at school and still remember today, and you'll see that most of the lines are around seven words. Where they're longer, another device is used to make them memorable.

A classic Bible quote
'In the beginning was the word, (6)
And the word was with God, (6)
And the word was God.' (5)
NOTE *the repetition of the two ideas 'the word' and 'God.'*

Jerusalem **by William Blake, poet**
'And did those feet in ancient time (7)
Walk up on England's mountains green? (6)
And was the holy lamb of God (6)
On England's pleasant pastures seen?' (5)
NOTE *the short lines, the use of repetition and rhyme and the way this 'paints a picture'.*

Jim, who ran away from his nurse and was eaten by a lion
by Hilaire Belloc (poet, essayist and commentator)
'There was a boy whose name was Jim. (8)
His friends were very good to him. (7)
They gave him tea and cakes and jam (8)
And slices of delicious ham ...' (5)
NOTE *the lines are short, the words simple, they rhyme, and are starting to create a picture.*

$5 not $15 words

When we use this metaphor in training it always seems to resonate. $5 words come from everyday language, writing as you speak, and using strong active language that creates a picture, such as 'laugh', 'dance', 'sing', 'swim', 'run', 'jump', 'walk'.

$15 words are usually technical, polysyllabic, frequently riddled with jargon and don't paint a picture. Some we've picked up from a recent speech are 'infrastructure', 'connecting', 'enabling', 'collaborating', 'providing', 'facilitating', 'conjoined services', 'digitization', 'obesogenic statistics' ... the list goes on.

If you're not familiar with it already, we recommend you support and adopt the key principles of the Plain English Campaign. Check out the website: www.plainenglish.co.uk

This is a worldwide movement that has been campaigning against gobbledygook, jargon and misleading public information since 1979. It also provides great resources and works with thousands of organizations to help them make their public information much clearer.

Here's the Plain English Campaign's basic list on clear writing.

- Keep your sentences short.
- Prefer active verbs.
- Use 'you' and 'we'.
- Use words that are appropriate for the reader.
- Don't be afraid to give instructions.

- Avoid nominalizations (turning verbs into nouns).
- Use lists where appropriate.

Here's a list of words frequently seen in speeches. See how easy it is to simplify them.

- additional (use 'extra')
- advise (use 'tell')
- applicant (use 'you')
- commence (use 'start')
- complete (use 'fill in')
- comply with (use 'keep to')
- consequently (use 'so')
- ensure (use 'make sure')
- forward (use 'send')
- in accordance with (use 'under, keeping to')
- in excess of (use 'more than')
- in respect of (use 'for')
- in the event of (use 'if')
- on receipt (use 'when we/you get')
- on request (use 'if you ask')
- particulars (use 'details')
- per annum (use 'a year')
- persons (use 'people')
- prior to (use 'before')
- purchase (use 'buy')
- regarding (use 'about')
- should you wish (use 'if you want')
- terminate (use 'end')
- whilst (use 'while')

Using statistics

'Don't be jealous if I spend 50 per cent of my time with you, and 50 per cent of my time with others, because you get 100 per cent of 50 per cent while all the others have to share that other 50 per cent.'

— Jarod Kintz, American author

Well-presented statistics can really be persuasive in a presentation. The trick is to select the best ones on your topic and align them with your key messages and stories. Sometimes statistics can provide a great opening for your presentation.

Jamie Oliver's 2012 Ted talk on YouTube, 'Teach Every Child About Food' shares powerful stories from his anti-obesity project in West Virginia.

This is his opening line: 'Sadly in the next 18 minutes, while I'm chatting to you, four Americans will be dead through the food they eat.'

Very quickly he uses another great statistic when he asks the audience how many of them have children? He tells them their children will have a life ten years shorter than theirs through eating bad food. (Check out his speech at http://www.ted.com/talks/jamie_oliver?language=en)

Use statistics selectively, get them right and display them well. Some very persuasive statistics appear on websites all over the internet, but it's important to check and double-check that any sources and statistics you find to back up your speech are accurate and come from reliable research.

Here's another interesting look at statistics that upstaged Jamie Oliver's claim that obesity is the biggest killer in the United States. This 2015 story in the US magazine *Mother Jones* presents a very convincing and well-researched case that gun violence is now killing more Americans than obesity. The website reference is: http://www.motherjones.com/politics/2015/04/true-cost-of-gun-violence-in-america

Endings — curtains fall

How do you want to be remembered? The ending is the opportunity to reinforce your key points. Take as much care with the end of your speech as with the beginning. Know your ending well. You have an opportunity to add value to people's lives. Don't waste that moment. Be memorable. Be sincere and be yourself.

One of the most powerful ways to end a speech or presentation is to finish with a great quote, even if it's from your grandmother or is an excerpt from a book that is relevant to the key message. Leave people feeling pleased they invested the time in listening to your presentation.

Tips for creative endings

- Finish with a great quote.
- Use a powerful analogy or metaphor.
- Tell a short story.
- Thank the audience.
- Sing a song — if you can sing.

TIPS ON WRITING YOUR SPEECH

- **Research your audience.**
- **Establish your purpose.** What do you want to achieve with the speech?
- **Develop a clear structure. Where do you intend to take your listeners?**
- Spend more time on your introduction and ending to create impact.
- **Stick to the allocated timing.**
- Think of your presentation as a conversation or a talk, not a formal speech.
- **Write with images or pictures in mind. Talk in pictures.**
- Avoid technical jargon. A twelve-year-old should be able to understand your speech.
- **Excite and stimulate your audience's imagination to gain their attention.**
- Share your stories — they are gold.

7
Honouring Your Audience

'The audience informs you of absolutely everything.'

— Dame Judy Dench, actor

Your audience is important. During an interview with Dame Judy Dench, an American student asked the great English thespian, 'Does the audience make a difference?' She responded, 'If an audience doesn't make any difference, I am staying at home and putting my feet up the chimney.'

We like people who are real. People will warm to you if you are authentic in your interaction with them. Your job is to make your audience comfortable and at ease so they will listen to every word you say.

I often use pre-course questionnaires and evaluation forms to ascertain the real concerns and fears of senior managers from global corporations about speaking to audiences large and small. Some of the most common responses are:

- I try to completely avoid speaking opportunities in front of audiences.
- I fear that I will be asked questions that I can't answer.
- I'm concerned that I lack impact and don't hold the attention of the audience.

- I fear that people are not listening or that they have checked out because I'm not impactful.
- If I'm unsure of a question, I don't have the confidence to ask the audience member to clarify what they mean.
- I worry that the audience will see me as passive, indecisive and lacking influence.
- I don't feel I have the skills to engage the audience, speak with authority and have presence at the table.

If you relate to any of these, trust me, you are not alone.

Connecting with your audience

'I'm looking for the truth. The audience doesn't come to see you, they come to see themselves.' — Julianne Moore, actor

Actors are driven to be creative and I have never met an actor who is not vulnerable in their life or on the stage. It is this vulnerability that allows actors to connect with their audience and draw us into the play.

Another valuable lesson I learnt from many years working in the theatre was to respect and honour the audience. Each person coming to see our show needed to get his or her money's worth. We owed it to the audience to get it right. They were coming night after night to watch and listen, learn, feel, be moved to tears or laughter and see their lives up there on a stage. We were always grateful to our audiences for supporting our productions and paying our salaries, and performed even if there were only a few people in the theatre.

Speaking to actor Alec Baldwin on his US radio show and podcast 'Here's the Thing', stand-up comedian Jerry Seinfeld shared his thoughts about connecting with his audience.

'You have this relationship with the audience that is private between you and them,' Seinfeld said. 'I don't "hang out" on stage. I'm up there to work. I am going to work for you because I respect this relationship and I want to keep it.'

Every time you present, ask yourself, 'Why am I doing this?' Find a reason other than financial reward or obligation. You have to speak from the heart and care about your audience in order to connect with it. One sentence could change someone's viewpoint forever.

> *'There is a difference between impressing an audience, and connecting with an audience. But once you have the connection, you can take them where you want to go.'*
> — Lilly Walters, author

You also need to not just respect but also accept your audience, no matter who they are. Failing to connect with the people sitting and listening to you can have embarrassing consequences. I have seen people fall asleep when a speaker lacks content or energy. I've also heard performers blame the audience for a bad presentation. If you are ever tempted to do this I suggest you re-examine why you accepted an invitation to speak in public in the first place. It's simply not fair to ask people to listen to a presenter who doesn't want to be there. If you look at a speaking gig as another boring or tiresome task, then the result will be just that.

So, while you can't always control the audience's response, you can do everything in your power to make sure people sit up and listen. As author Brian Tracy so aptly says, 'You get them to like you by showing them that it is an honour to be with them.'

Timing

Timing is a key ingredient in connecting with your audience. According to an article from Columbia University's Graduate School of Arts and Science Teaching Center, 'The first 30 seconds have the most impact.' The start of your speech needs to grab the audience's attention. Creating a response and building a relationship relies on you developing rapport, so you can then begin to communicate effectively.

But, beware, because you can lose that rapport just as quickly as you won it if you start to meander and go over time. In all my reading, research and through personal experience I have discovered that an audience can only concentrate for 20 minutes through a speech.

I attended a one-day conference where there were a number of guest speakers who all went over time, despite the many failed attempts by the MC to rein them in. This went on for hours. The audience (including me) was fidgeting and struggling to absorb the content, and although we desperately needed a drink and a snack, by the time cocktail hour arrived, organizers faced a speedy exodus from a crowd just itching to get home. The lesson here is that if you don't respect timing, an audience will lose respect for you.

Encore! Encore!

The French have introduced us to *Encore! Encore!* 'Again, some more!' I have stood up with others and cheered and stamped my feet wanting more when a speaker or singer has been brilliant. When you next give a speech think back to all those events where you've wanted to hear more and try to analyze why these presenters have captured your heart and soul.

Charisma

Experts say that our minds tend to 'drift' 47 per cent of the time. This can happen for many reasons such as stress, tiredness and distraction. If this is true you need to find a way of holding the audience in the palm of your hand. Clients are always asking me if one can learn to be charismatic. My answer has always been, yes, anything is possible. I have witnessed many miracles over the past 30 years. The qualities I look for in a charismatic speaker are kindness, warmth, strength and self-belief.

> *'Personality is the glitter that sends your little gleam across the footlights and the orchestra pit into that big black space where the audience is.'* — Mae West, actor

If you allow your true personality to shine, your speech will be memorable and your audience will talk about you for years. As they say in the theatre, you're only as good as your last gig.

Get the audience involved

'The audience will only be interested in sincerity not tricks.' — Raymond Hawthorne, actor and playwright

My clients are often afraid of introducing audience participation into their speech because it involves risk, experimentation and getting involved with the people they are speaking to. It also makes some speakers feel very vulnerable.

How to gain an audience's trust

'My job is to step into the room and capture every soul.'
— Tony Robbins, motivational speaker

For an audience to trust you, you must first trust in what you are saying and have confidence in yourself. An audience will never respond if you project a lack of confidence. Superstar speakers like Bill Clinton are in demand because they have an inner confidence when they take the stage or podium.

Learning to trust an audience simply takes time and practice. Interact with your audience. They are not separate; they are a part of your communication, your speech or your business presentation. It has to be a two-way conversation even if you are the only one speaking. Interact with them so they are fully engaged. Communication is like a dance. It must involve movement, back and forth, a flow of energy and dialogue.

Here are some different ways to engage with an audience:

- **Physically.** If you are speaking to a small group, greet them individually with a warm handshake and a personal smile. If you're speaking to a larger group, greet at least a few of the audience before the presentation. This will put you at ease.
- **Verbally.** When addressing the group, speak as though you're talking to a group of friends, not strangers.
- **Mentally.** Know in your heart that this audience wants you to succeed. They never want you to fail. Don't doubt; believe in yourself.

- **Content.** Understand why the audience has come to hear you and make sure your messages are clear.
- **Interaction.** Ask questions and get your audience involved during and at the end of your speech.

What does your audience need and expect from you?

Here's my checklist of qualities that matter when addressing an audience:

A — Attitude

U — Unity

D — Direction

I — Involvement

E — Empathy

N — Nurturing

C — Credibility

E — Enthusiasm

ATTITUDE

> *'My personality is 90 per cent attitude.'*
> — Elwood N. Chapman, author

A positive attitude is the most important quality any communicator can have. Your audience will be more attentive and energetic, and will respect you for your great outlook on life. If you're angry or upset, don't speak to an audience — the response will be negative and your body language will ultimately give you away.

TIPS

- Smile and you will start to feel more positive.
- Remove all negative chatter and thoughts from your mind when you speak.

- Every time you blame or put yourself down, stop — pause and replace it with a positive thought.
- Research different styles of behaviour so you can understand your moods and change habits.

UNITY

> *'You have to respect your audience. Without them, you're essentially standing alone, singing to yourself.'*
> — K.D. Lang, singer

Your job is to bring your audience together so you can establish two-way communication. It's about making people feel part of a community.

TIPS

- Ask questions. A question at the beginning is a good way to open a presentation.
- Involve them. You are delivering a speech but there is still space for participation.
- Plant someone in the audience to ask the first question. This gives others the confidence to ask questions as well.

DIRECTION

You have a responsibility to know where you are taking your audience. Direct them on a carefully mapped-out route, so they are not confused about your message.

People always want to know there is a purpose to what they are listening to. It is a simple route: the audience needs a beginning, middle and an end to the presentation in order to understand it.

TIPS

- Have a beginning, middle and an end to your speech.
- Give an overview at the beginning so the audience knows where you are leading them.

ır key points at the end to remind them of
 heard.

que ending that is easy for your audience

If you have the courage to be different you will have more chance of getting an audience's attention. Many of my clients have been afraid to use
interactive exercises in a presentation. But the only way you are going to
find out if it works is to do it. I don't know how many times I have
received a phone call saying, 'I tried it and it worked!'

People learn best in an experiential environment. The simplest way of
involving an audience is by asking questions and getting them talking so
that the communication is two-way. Try to think of activities that will
enhance the messages you are communicating to your audience. I interrupt most of my speeches with an interactive exercise to make a point and
to energize the audience.

TIPS

- Ask the audience to think of a story relevant to the theme
  of the presentation. Tell them to turn to their neighbour
  and share it.
- Introduce an energizer; get everyone up on their feet.
  It must be relevant to the theme.
- Hire actors to improvise or act out a scenario.
- Invite a surprise guest and get the audience to anticipate
  who is turning up.
- Personally acknowledge audience members. I do this by
  giving a signed book away at presentations to someone
  who has participated in an exercise on stage or even who
  has a birthday that day.

EMPATHY

Empathy is the ability to walk in someone else's shoes. I put myself in
someone else's world to try to find a way of understanding their viewpoint

and feelings — to be empathetic. The older I get, the less judgmental I am because I work really hard on developing this quality. This is one of the most essential tools in communication. Never put down, blame or judge your audience. Share your experiences so they will get to know you.

We learn to be empathetic by listening and observing others. It is an essential interpersonal skill no matter where you work or what you do.

TIPS

- People need to know you are hearing them. But never say, 'I know how you feel' — because you don't.
- Observe people's body language for unspoken messages about how they're feeling.
- Take time to stop and to listen to people.

NURTURING

'When I come into the theatre I get a sense of security. I love an audience. I love people, and I act because I like trying to give pleasure to people.' — Vivien Leigh, actor

It's the presenter's responsibility to nurture their audience and to take care of them no matter what the subject matter. He or she enables the audience to learn. Deepak Chopra, the famous author, is a master at nurturing his audience. I remember sitting in an auditorium fascinated by his caring nature as he walked the length of the stage. The warm tone in his voice made me feel as though he was talking directly to me and personally invested in my growth.

TIPS

- Nurture yourself first, then attend to the audience.
- Speak with a caring tone in your voice.
- Kindness doesn't cost, so be generous with it.

One way of showing that you care is to stay around after your speech is over to listen to people's questions and engage with them.

Check your audience is physically comfortable; for example, ask if the room temperature is OK. (See Chapter 13 on setting the stage for further ideas.)

CREDIBILITY

Your audience needs to believe you from the moment you open your mouth. You are the expert in your field and that's why you are speaking to this audience. Without credibility your message will have no impact. Don't be afraid to let your audience know why you are the best person to speak to them on a topic. For example, if you're speaking about sales techniques because you've been your company's top sales rep for the past year, make sure that the audience know this either through your speech or through the person who introduces you. This gives the audience a reason to trust you and your message.

Your reputation is important. Being introduced at the beginning of your presentation is vital as it establishes your credibility. The MC needs to know if there is any information you would like them to tell the audience before you start speaking.

TIPS

- Provide the person introducing you with relevant, up-to-date material and credentials well in advance. Let them know how you'd like to be introduced.

- If possible try to meet the person introducing you so they get a sense of who you are. You can also provide them with anecdotes about you that could be shared with the audience to evoke authority and intimacy.

- Don't be afraid to tell people about your skills. What is your claim to fame?

ENTHUSIASM

Enthusiasm is essential to wake up any audience and keep their interest. You cannot have too much passion. I ask every new client, 'What are you passionate about?' This forms the basis of my approach in coaching so I can tap into what matters to them. Depriving your audience of your enthusiasm robs them of any relationship with you. Audiences will forgive you almost anything if you are wholehearted and share your inner beliefs.

Who are your favourite speakers? I guarantee they display eagerness and zest. Enthusiasm comes from loving what you do, so be passionately purposeful and upbeat when presenting to a group.

TIPS

- Practise being positive in your private life and it will spill over into your professional life and work presentations.
- Look at the company you keep and surround yourself with enthusiastic people. It rubs off.
- Talk about something you are passionate about. If your material is dry, boring and dull to you, then how can you expect your audience to get excited about it? Tell stories that fire you up.
- Confident posture, a smile, energy and a lively voice tell your audience you are enthusiastic.

Warming up the crowd

Many years of experience working as a professional MC have taught me how important it is to read the audience carefully. It is crucial to be adaptable and flexible with a crowd. Don't be afraid of things going wrong. Two-way communication is about mutual understanding. What is your audience feeling and thinking? What is the mood or atmosphere telling you? Are they relaxed, shy, receptive, defensive, angry or cynical?

Some suggestions for warming up the crowd include:

- Bring spot prizes to give away, such as a book, voucher or movie ticket. Make it relevant to the presentation's theme.
- Challenge the audience to fun and spontaneous competitions. You could try asking some questions and have a prize for the winner.

Heckling

'Don't forget that your audience has rights too. They have the right to hear you clearly, see you, be moved to tears or laughter or anger by what you say, be inspired and ultimately to boo you, if they wish.'
— Witi Ihimaera, author of *The Whale Rider*

Even the best presenters have to deal with hecklers at times — people who either disagree with what you're saying or just want to disrupt the speech or show off. Don't take it personally, and above all, stay calm. Hecklers usually annoy the rest of the audience and you may find that someone else in the audience asks them to be quiet on your behalf. Some of my strategies for dealing with hecklers are:

- In the first instance, try to ignore them. If it's a one-off comment that doesn't merit a response, continue with your presentation. Break eye contact with the person. If the audience can see you're not paying any attention to the heckler, neither will they.

- If the heckler is intent on attracting your attention to make their point, I don't recommend trying to heckle back. You'll just get drawn into a slanging match. Stay polite and the audience will be on your side.

- You could try a comment such as, 'We have a lot of material to cover and I'd rather not get off track, so how about at the break we get together and talk about this?' Hopefully, the heckler will understand this as a request to tone it down.

- Another approach is to acknowledge the heckler's point of view with a comment such as 'That's one way to look at it,' or, 'I can see why you might think that, but consider looking at it this way.' If they really persist, ask the audience, 'Is anyone else having difficulty with this point?' If the answer is no, suggest to the heckler that you continue the conversation during the break.

If a couple of people are talking through your presentation, ask them a question or just stop and wait for them to finish. If someone starts talking on a mobile phone, ask them politely to please leave the presentation and carry on their conversation outside.

> 'He aha the mea nui?'
> (What is the most important thing?)
> 'He tāngata, he tāngata, he tāngata!'
> (It's people, people, people.)
> — Maori proverb

TIPS ON MANAGING YOUR AUDIENCE

- **Credibility is crucial — let your audience know why you've been asked to speak to them. Your MC can also do this for you.**

- Your audience wants you to succeed — they're on your side.

- **Energize your audience. Consider an interactive activity at the beginning or part way through your speech.**

- Gifts and prizes can be a fun icebreaker.

- **Smile! Your enthusiasm will be contagious — show you're enjoying yourself and your audience will too.**

- Look at your audience, not the floor. Build rapport by making eye contact.

- **Take risks — let your audience know who you are and what you stand for. Be prepared to step outside your comfort zone.**

- Ask experienced trainers for help. Borrow exercises and activities that have a proven record in order to enliven your presentation.

8
Warming Up

'The fastest way to still your mind is to move your body.'

— Gabrielle Roth, dance theatre artist

Warming up helps to focus the mind and body on the task ahead. Completing a warm-up before a presentation will ensure that you are concentrating on the right things, your vocal cords are ready for action and you are relaxed and confident about the speaking engagement. Just as you wouldn't go for a run without first warming up your muscles, or just as actors wouldn't warm-up before a theatre performance, public speakers don't perform without first ensuring that they are ready to give 100 per cent from the very beginning of the presentation.

On the few occasions where I haven't taken the time to properly warm-up I have been unhappy with my performance. If you're not ready to perform before starting your speech it will take the crucial first minutes of your presentation before you really get into the swing of things and, by then, you may have lost the audience's attention.

Take a lesson from the sports stars

In my view, the *haka* performed by the All Blacks before a rugby test match is the most powerful public warm-up that integrates body, voice, mind and spirit. The players get so fired up during this ritual. Former All Black Stu Wilson recalls the importance of the *haka* to the team's pre-match routine. 'We knew we were likely to get smashed if we didn't warm up properly. If the *haka* was done well, I could tell the boys were going to play well. The opposition were in trouble. The *haka* put them at a disadvantage — they sometimes turned their back on us because they felt challenged. The *haka* gave us instant recognition — it was like the opening of the performance, just like the opening line in a speech.'

There are many similarities between theatre and sports. Shelley McMeeken, former CEO of Netball New Zealand, comments, 'One of the compelling things about netball is its unpredictability. It's like unprescribed theatre such as theatresports where the athletes [actors] are part of an unpredictable story line.' Sportspeople wouldn't dream of competing without adequate preparation; it becomes part of their routine. They know that they don't perform to the best of their ability if their mind and body are not ready for action.

Shelley describes her warm-up routine for press interviews. 'For us to be successful we have to win on and off the court. The players warm-up before a big game and equally I warm-up prior to a press conference or interview by visualizing what tactics I may have to counter. Our Silver Ferns don't go on unprepared when they represent our organization and nor should I.'

Do what works for you

Warm-ups are very personal — try different activities until you find something that clicks. Sometimes I listen to upbeat music if I am giving an early evening speech at cocktail hour. I have even been known to dance around the conference room in full view of technicians and hotel staff. The goal is to get the blood flowing and the brain focused on the presentation. Experiment and talk to friends about their warm-up routines.

One of the more unusual warm-up routines I've seen is that advocated by Ross Foreman, one of Australasia's most successful auctioneers. I co-facilitated a workshop with him training auctioneers to perform more effectively. Auctioneers are very aware of the need to warm up before performing because of the stress they place on their voices. The auction process is very theatrical and relies on a powerful performance with a strong voice and the familiar fast rhythm. He used to ask each auctioneer to hold a chair as though it was a set of bagpipes and to walk around the room making rhythmical sounds! Taking people out of their comfort zones in a non-threatening way broke down barriers and helped to build their confidence. Ross also liked to use poetry and excerpts from plays as part of the auctioneers' warm-up programme. The participants would stand outside under the trees and practise projecting their voices. We also used improvisation and theatre-style vocal exercises.

I remember one excellent auctioneer who was named Auctioneer of the Year several years in a row in Australia. One year when he didn't win the title, he confessed that he hadn't warmed up his voice or been through his standard set of relaxation exercises before the competition.

Routine

We prepare for most things in life. We have rituals before we go to work, go to the gym, cook a meal. Brushing our teeth in the morning is a part of preparing for the day. Stretching before exercising is another preparation.

Incorporate small exercises into your pre-presentation routine and always warm-up before you speak. If you are reluctant to do this ask yourself why. Is it because you don't know what to do or can't find a quiet room or space? Perhaps you feel stupid or believe it won't make a difference. Maybe you can't be bothered. With positive self-talk and a commitment to delivering a first-class presentation to your audience you will find ways to deal with these doubts.

I often warm up in the venue one hour before a speech. If working with a client I make sure I am also there to help them warm up. Find someone to support you during your warm-up exercises to make sure you do them.

Warm-ups can be a combination of any or all of the following activities: going to the gym, walking, singing, meditating, praying, using positive self-talk, practising a few yoga postures or a warm-up of your own choice before the performance. There are suggestions later in this chapter of particular exercises you might like to try, but the main thing is to find a warm-up that works for you, that you feel comfortable with, and that gets you physically and mentally ready to give a great presentation.

Don't just warm up for a public speech. Even interviews and salary negotiations are performances that require you to be on your toes and focused. Make limbering up a habit; it will eventually start to become a ritual for you until you cannot imagine speaking to a group without going through your routine.

How long should I take?

Warm-ups can last from 5 minutes to one hour, depending on how much time you can spare or how experienced you are at speaking in public. Make an appointment with yourself to do some kind of physical and vocal practice before your next presentation, even a quick walk around the block — anything to get the blood pumping.

Ask a friend or colleague to monitor you if you are struggling to be disciplined. Set up a buddy system so you can return the favour. Motivate them and help them to remove some of the stress around their presentation.

Suggestions for your warm-up routine

Breathing

We often take breathing for granted yet the quality of our breath determines the quality of our speech.

Try to avoid shallow breathing, which occurs when you raise your shoulders but your lungs aren't given enough room to expand. Shallow breathing means we don't get enough air to finish a sentence. If you have to stop for breath in the middle of a sentence, it is likely that you're not breathing deeply enough. The goal is to speak so your sentences flow from one to the other.

> 'Warm-ups are only useful if you do them regularly.'
> — Miranda Harcourt, actor

In yoga every movement is led by the breath. Many years ago I attended a two-day workshop with one of the world's top yoga teachers, Desikachar, author of the classic yoga text *The Heart of Yoga*. He says, 'There are many interpretations of the word yoga that have been handed down over the centuries. One of these is to come together, to unite. Another meaning of the word yoga is to tie the strands of the mind together.'

I love the latter expression; knowing the meaning behind the word 'yoga' helps to understand why it can be a helpful tool in your warm-up routine.

Every time you experience stage fright, breathe deeply in and out and eventually you will relax. I practise yoga breathing exercises before a presentation.

Sallie-Ann Stones, yoga teacher, talks about the benefits of yoga in her life. 'The practice of yoga has given me a greater understanding of my possibilities and most importantly, myself, my capabilities and my limitations. It has been a tool of growth — as my body has become stronger and more flexible and re-aligned itself from past habits, I have observed that my mental and emotional states have followed suit. As my breath has deepened, so has my thinking. As my energy has increased, so has my interest in life. As I've become more comfortable and at ease in my body it has become more natural and easy to stand up and be who I am.'

Do consider attending a yoga class to improve your breathing habits. If you have difficulty breathing, I highly recommend Dinah Bradley's book *Hyperventilation Syndrome* to increase your understanding of your breathing patterns. Learning to breathe correctly will enable you to release the stress in your body. I often practise these exercises when I am tired or between client sessions to get more oxygen to my brain and to feel rejuvenated.

EXERCISE

Stand with your feet shoulder-width apart and place the palms of your hands on your lower abdomen. Close your eyes, inhaling your breath through your nose, expanding your abdomen. Raise your arms, moving them outward and above your head. Hold for a count of five, and then exhale slowly, breathing through your nose, lowering your arms. Repeat five times.

EXERCISE

Start by sitting comfortably, with your spine straight and your eyes and mouth gently closed. Relax your head and shoulders; relax your face and your jaw. Become aware of the flow of your own natural breath, in

and out of the nostrils, without controlling or changing it in any way, just observing it and watching. Continue this until your whole mind is full of just breathing in and breathing out.

Bring your awareness to your abdomen. Imagine you have a balloon in your belly and when you breathe in fill this balloon with air. Hold the breath there, in your belly, and feel as though you are absorbing the breath deep inside yourself. If you have a particular area of pain or discomfort, imagine you are sending the breath there. Hold it only as long as you comfortably can, then release the breath. When breathing out, also release any tensions and any physical, mental or emotional negativity.

Continue for several breaths. Simply observe your natural flow of breath see how subtle your breath has become. Notice any changes within yourself and your physical and mental wellbeing.

EXERCISE

Judy Apps' excellent book *Voice and Speaking Skills for Dummies* is full of simple, practical advice for warming up the voice. This is her exercise for warming up the jaw. 'You need to be able to release the jaw and move it freely. So just feel it flop open. Imagine that you're a fish and open and close your mouth in the same soft, pouty way. Hear your lips give a satisfying popping sound as you release the jaw. Check that your back teeth are separated, which is a good indicator that you've released your jaw.'

> '*A little vocal preparation can be the difference between a voice that trudges along with a slouching tread, or one that swings easily and gracefully in a confident stride.*'
> — Judy Apps, author and voice tutor

Get moving to release tension

Tension in the body when speaking is largely the result of not doing a warm-up. It's not enough to just rely on the message and words you're delivering — your body has to look as if it believes the words coming from your mouth. Where is the tension in your body?

We need to get our blood and oxygen flowing to wake up. We cannot expect our listeners to be alert if we are sluggish. Fresh air is free and energizes your body. Surrendering tension invigorates your performance. What does it really mean to let the tension go? How do you like to let go? It is different for every person. For me, dancing, running on a beach, meditating, singing and laughing are all ways that I let go.

I try to spend time outside in between clients; it makes all the difference to my energy levels. Even 5 minutes outside peps up your body and gives you a lift.

Any movement will help you to focus. Practise your golf swing or your tennis serve. Use exercises you enjoy; don't allow it to become a chore.

Many of you will play sport and have your own particular warm-up. What do you do to warm up before delivering a presentation? Make up your own routine that you can easily remember and structure it accordingly. It doesn't matter if you walk, move, dance or stretch, just get into a regular habit of moving.

> *'Warming up will make your performances better.'*
> — Eric Barr, teacher of acting and directing, University of California

EXERCISE

Start from your head and work down to your shoulders then to your arms, chest, hips, legs and feet. Move each body part, slowly rolling and stretching. Make soft gentle fluid movements that make you feel more relaxed.

EXERCISE

Ben Cole, who teaches public speaking in London to film actors and directors at the National Film School, talks about what happens when we panic and stop moving easily. 'There is a ball and socket joint at the top of the spine and you can't think clearly unless you are moving it.' He suggests that 10 seconds before you speak, stand in front of the audience, start to slightly move your head, looking at the audience and making eye contact. Breathe deeply, wait for the right words to come out. Don't rush into speaking before you're ready. Don't make obvious movements, but slowly and naturally ease yourself into a comfortable speaking position instead of keeping your head still.

EXERCISE

If you suffer back pain, try the following. Lie on your back and bring both of your knees to your chest. Gently squeeze your legs. Move slowly from side to side with no great effort. This will massage your back and will stretch your lower back muscles.

Releasing tension in the voice and face

Chapter 4 has many suggestions for improving and maintaining your voice. Here are some exercises for warming up the face and vocal cords before your presentation.

EXERCISE

Gargle a glass of water while singing a scale in the back of your throat as loudly as you can.

EXERCISE

To release tension in the mouth, try this horse-lips exercise. Blow air out through your mouth as if you are blowing raspberries on a baby's tummy. You might prefer to be somewhere private when you try this one! Loose relaxed lips are what we are aiming for as opposed to tight ones.

EXERCISE

Here's another exercise for releasing tension in your face. Let your tongue sit comfortably in your mouth, and blow some air through your lips in a repetitive motion. Now add some sound and increase the volume. Your face may tingle when you do this.

Loosen your jaw with the following exercises. Open your mouth and move your jaw from right to left. Open your mouth wide then close. Pretend you are yawning. Repeat.

EXERCISE

These tongue twisters will help to sharpen your diction. Repeat each phrase five times.

- Unique New York
- Red leather yellow leather
- Red lorry yellow lorry
- Will you wait for William and Willy
- She sells seashells on the seashore
- Around the rugged rocks the ragged rascal ran

EXERCISE

To improve resonance in your voice, try humming for three minutes or until your lips tingle, remembering to breathe. Many opera singers hum before a performance. You can even hum in the car, although it's preferable to set aside time to perform all exercises closer to the time you are actually speaking.

EXERCISE

Sing your favourite song. You are exercising the mouth, lips, tongue, jaw and facial muscles as well as your vocal cords. Singing also makes you feel good. No need to get hung up on staying in tune; choose a song you enjoy.

EXERCISE

Reading aloud is an excellent way to warm up your vocal cords. Practise reading as if your audience were sitting across from you at the table, then across the room, then across the street.

Warming up the mind

Concentrate on staying positive before your presentation, trying to remove all negative thoughts from your mind. Let go of all judgments you have about yourself and your audience before you stand up and speak. Release any preconceived ideas about the event that's about to happen. If you resent your boss, for example, because she has insisted you make a speech when you don't want to, let go of that thought and attitude. You don't need it and it will only hinder the quality of your performance.

Chapter 11 on transforming fear with self-belief has a comprehensive section on using visualization and affirmations to prepare your mind for speaking in public.

EXERCISE

Try listening to relaxing music for a week leading up to an important speech. Take an iPod, iPad, laptop, whatever device you use to the venue to select music according to your needs. Classical music calms me before a speech and stops me worrying about the outcome. If I'm tired I select something more upbeat.

A SAMPLE WARM-UP PROGRAMME

- Stretch your body out, by dancing or jogging to music. Try a few yoga stretches or walk around the block. Get the heart going!
- Align your body. Imagine a piece of string running through your head, down the back of your neck and down your spine. Turn your head gently to the left, back to the centre, then to the right. Repeat 10 times.
- Roll your shoulders gently forward and back, then pull your shoulders up to your ears then relax. Repeat each action 10 times.
- Control your breathing. Put a hand on your stomache, breathe in deeply through your nose all the way to your hand. Keep your shoulders relaxed.
- Relax. Breathe in through your nose then breathe out through your open mouth. Pause. Repeat, making an

'ahhh' sound on the exhalation. Pause. Be aware of releasing any tension in your body. Breathe slowly, so as not to hyperventilate, then on the next exhalation, let out an easy laugh, then a 'hmmmm' sound, then hum up and down the scale.

- Have a gargle in the bathroom. Stand tall. Breathe easy.
- Warm-up your face. Screw your face up and vigorously chew on a piece of imaginary gum. Massage your face. Vibrate your lips like a horse, making a 'ppprrrrr' sound. Try the following sounds:
    - ptk ptk ptk ptk
    - bdg bdg bdg bdg
    - ing ah ing ah ing ah ing ah
- Tongue twisters. Try some of the following:
    - Little Lillian, living by the lily pond, lets lazy lizards lie along the lily pads.
    - Zena, the zenith zebra, lives life with zestful zeal.
    - Lips tongue tip of the teeth (repeat 5 times).
    - Articulatory agility is a desirable ability manipulating with dexterity the tongue, the palate and the lips.
- Close your eyes and visualize yourself giving your presentation. Visualize being introduced, walking to the podium, acknowledging the audience, enjoying delivering your speech, seeing the audience enjoying listening to it, hearing the rousing applause and walking off the stage after a successful speech.
- Use positive self-talk and affirmations, such as, 'The audience wants to listen to me.'
- Sing a song.
- Enjoy yourself.

TIPS ON WARMING UP

- Set up a regular time before your speech to warm up in a quiet place.
- Use music to relax and energize yourself during your warm-up routine. An iPod can be handy.
- Get out of the office or the venue where you're speaking and breathe in some fresh air.
- Take long deep breaths until you feel your body relaxing.

9

The Rehearsal

'The rehearsal is the place to take risks and to find out how far you can go. You must consider it is the safest place for you to push yourself and make a fool of yourself. Practise and prepare for the rehearsal before you arrive. Don't come to the rehearsal and start doing your homework.' — Michael Hurst, actor

A rehearsal is the place to experiment. It's the creative process, a time to take risks. A rehearsal is an opportunity to try out ideas, test yourself and seek feedback. A satisfactory rehearsal gives you a sense of confidence and makes you feel positive about your upcoming speech or presentation.

For many, the rehearsal is a new concept especially when it comes to business pitches or presentations. But every speech deserves a rehearsal even if it's a simple 5-minute presentation because it is a reflection on you. If you are careless and ambivalent you will be unmemorable.

I don't believe that there is any such thing as failure in a rehearsal. It's better to experiment and make mistakes at a rehearsal than during the presentation. If you are telling a story, a joke, using visuals or introducing a prop for the first time you can get feedback from your colleagues, friends, family or test audience. I have seen people cry during a rehearsal from sheer frustration and embarrassment — better it happens at the rehearsal. The more mistakes you make, the better your presentation or speech will be.

The biggest excuse I hear from my clients is, 'I can't rehearse, I'm not ready and I haven't got the time.' My answer to my clients is to make the time. I'm known for my tough love. An athlete shows up every day unless he or she has a serious injury. And even then they continue to do everything they possibly can to get back into the game.

Rehearse until you get it right. No cutting corners, no tricks, no winging it on the day. Never delay or cancel a rehearsal. Even the most experienced and high profile presenters rehearse when it matters. And never underestimate the importance of the rehearsal, even if you only have a few hours. If you're one of these people who leaves it to the last minute, bring someone in to critically assess and support you but do not have unrealistic expectations of yourself.

I was rehearsing with a client the day before he was to give an on-camera speech making an announcement to his staff. We spent almost two hours working on his message and delivery. If we had not done this work, he would have turned up well prepared with his content but the delivery could have been flat. Seeing his natural delivery at the end of the session was re-affirming.

> 'When I was younger, I never wanted to rehearse because I thought that someone would figure out I don't know what I'm doing. Now I like to really spend the time and figure it out and rehearsal is to try something that doesn't work.' — William Fichtner, actor

Winging it

I could not possibly count how many times a client has told me over the years that they 'winged it'. Manage your calendar around a major speech or presentation so you take responsibility. If you don't do this you run the risk of letting yourself down and knowing that you could have done better. It's not a satisfying feeling knowing that the audience didn't connect and respond. Your integrity will also suffer as a result. If you prepare well in advance you can at least look yourself in the eye in the mirror and tell yourself, 'I did my best.'

Schedule

The number of rehearsals you choose will depend on the presentation, your expertise and your knowledge. I suggest to clients that they set aside at least four rehearsals for a major speech and start thinking about it months in advance if it's a large business audience. This gives time for research, enables creativity in content and helps to build confidence. One rehearsal is never sufficient. And remember it's important to come prepared to a rehearsal. Know your material and bring any props, PowerPoint slides or visual aids finished with you. If you are going to be using a lectern on the big day, hire one for your rehearsal.

Curtain rises

Can you imagine an actor or opera singer performing without a rehearsal? It just wouldn't happen. My work in professional theatre taught me that the audience must come first. They will never know the sacrifice and investment made for your speech, and this is how it should be. They are the focus and they deserve a fresh, powerful performance from you — no matter what your status or who you are.

Even the British Royals rehearse. It's public knowledge that Anthony Gordon Lennox, a former BBC Producer, taught the Duchess of Cambridge breathing techniques before her wedding. She wanted her performance to be perfect on the most important day of her life — for her and her audience. On her wedding day she had an audience of hundreds of millions and spoke confidently and remembered her lines.

> 'I love the rehearsal process in the theatre, and the visceral sense of contact and communication with a live audience.' — Judd Nelson, actor

Attitude

We are more creative when we are positive and more likely to encourage and embrace constructive criticism. But we all have our bad days, which are often the result of acute stress. Just be aware that if you bring a bad mood into the rehearsal space, morale for everyone suffers.

Frequently we set ourselves up for failure before we even start. Worrying before or during a rehearsal will not help you to prepare for your performance. If you're rehearsing with your colleagues, be supportive towards them. We can become overly absorbed in our own performance but we need to be aware of others in the rehearsal and consider our attitudes toward them.

Quick tips to manage your attitude

- Go for a quick walk outside in the fresh air.
- Take deep breaths, concentrating on exhaling and inhaling.
- Smile and think positive thoughts.
- Take a break and be nice to yourself.
- Put it in perspective.

'Attitude is a little thing that makes a big difference.'
— Winston Churchill, prime minister, orator and historian

Feedback

People can be at their most vulnerable during rehearsals, especially when a coach has been hired to critique them. It's not easy to be given feedback in front of others — especially by a stranger. My motto is always to leave people feeling great. People often do not think about the impact of what they say to others.

Fresh Eyre courses stand or fall on our ability to provide consistent high-quality feedback. We role model this in all our teaching practices; it is a priority for us. I come from the school of hard knocks in the theatre and at times I felt like I was in the army with directors yelling at me. I have spent years studying how to give constructive feedback, which has made such a difference to me as an accomplished trainer.

Giving and receiving feedback

High-quality feedback is central to honest working relationships. Your feedback can enhance or crush someone within minutes, so give it wisely and with integrity.

When giving feedback remember the following:

- Always try to maintain the self-esteem of the person you are giving feedback to.
- Focus on the behaviour, not the person.
- Refer to specific situations or facts — pinpoint specific behaviour you've noticed.
- Discuss why you think something was or was not effective.
- Reward behaviour you want to reinforce or suggest another way of doing things.
- Different people have different needs, so remember personality styles when giving your feedback.

Tips for effective feedback

- Be prepared to give both positive and negative feedback — but separate the two.
- Use unemotional, neutral language.
- Focus on things that others can do something about.
- Stick to the facts.
- Use 'I' statements.
- Avoid labels and judgments.
- Ask yourself: if you were receiving the feedback how would you like to receive it?

Tips for receiving feedback

- Centre yourself.
- Listen carefully.
- Ask questions.
- Acknowledge the feedback.
- Consider your response.

- Accept or reject the feedback.
- Affirm yourself.
- Manage your listening when you are given criticism and try not to take it personally.

See Chapter 18 for more tips on giving constructive feedback.

The read-through

In the theatre, actors have a read-through when they first come together, then begin performing at the second or third rehearsal without their script in their hands. During this rehearsal, actors arrive knowing their lines; if they don't, they find themselves in big trouble, having let down the cast and wasted the director's time. After four to five weeks they have a dress rehearsal and a technical rehearsal. In business I follow the same procedure with my clients and educate them to change their ways if this is not their current routine. It always pays off.

Timing is everything

The first question you need to ask is how long am I speaking for? It is fundamental to the planning, writing and rehearsing process. Someone needs to act as timekeeper. From my point of view, I think an hour is too long for a speech unless the person is a star performer. My preference is to speak for 20 minutes to half an hour and then open the floor to questions and answers before wrapping it up. If your speech is longer than an hour, consider giving your audience a short break. Never go over time, as this is disrespectful to your audience. If your audience does want to hear more from you, it is best to check if there is any extra time available with your organizers.

I've seen people speed up if the speaker before them has gone over time. This often happens in panel discussions with audiences. I remember sitting in the front row at a conference as a successful entrepreneur raced through her delivery. I felt absolutely exhausted by the time she had finished. The woman next to me kept asking me what she was saying because she was also mumbling her words. We missed out on some valuable stories and details. What the speaker needed to do was ask the Master of Ceremonies for more time or edit down some of her material.

Recording your speech

The camera doesn't lie. Our masterful camera people film all our clients so they can see their progress and take away a recording of the presentation.

I was rehearsing with an author who wanted to practise her first paid speech. Her book was about to be launched and she wanted to work with a professional. Like thousands of other clients, at first she didn't see the importance of being filmed. Eventually she could see that this was the only way to improve her presentation. Filming your speech during a rehearsal is an excellent way to see yourself as the audience will see you. It's an opportunity to notice your hand gestures, your speech inflections and to be aware of how confident you sound.

Visualize your performance

Visualization is achieved through using your imagination. One of the reasons I rehearse and go to check out the venue before a speech is because I want to visualize the audience in that room before I turn up for the event. Refer to Chapter 11 for more information on how to visualize your speech.

> '*I am a big believer in visualization. I run through my races mentally so that I feel even more prepared.*'
> — Allyson Felix, track-and-field sprint athlete

The dress rehearsal

The dress rehearsal is your last chance to get everything right. Better to find out during the dress rehearsal that the lapel microphone doesn't work or something in the room could distract you from your delivery, than at the performance. Are you dressed appropriately and wearing the clothing you will wear on the day? I often ask my clients to wear their suit or dress and film it so they can make sure that they are happy with their appearance.

A crucial element of the dress rehearsal is to ensure that all technology is working as you expect. Don't forget to check the position where you intend to deliver your presentation or speech. Are you blocking the screen from the audience?

I attended a business presentation with an interesting line up of speakers. It was a high-profile, international company with offices around the world. Some of its staff was observing via a video conferencing platform and all the speakers had lapel microphones, including the MC. About 15 minutes in, there was a screaming sound that lasted for about a minute. Clearly it was caused by a problem with the technology. The technician was running around trying to solve the problem. Eventually everything came right but the staff offsite could no longer hear the speakers. Needless to say, the chief executive who was on the panel was not impressed!

Sometimes things can go wrong when using technology even after you've had a dress rehearsal. It's important in your planning to work through every scenario so that you always have a back-up plan and you're not startled when there is a hiccup.

Translation

Another important thing to check is whether a translator or a sign language interpreter for the deaf will be participating in your presentation. This could well change your performance, so you must include it in your rehearsal. I learned this lesson when I was asked to speak at an event for a visiting Chinese government delegation. I hadn't thought to ask if there would be a translator or indeed whether the visitors had a good understanding of English. I was slightly thrown when I realized I would be working with a translator, who would repeat every sentence in Mandarin. I knew this would completely alter my presentation.

Luckily my acting skills really came in handy and I adopted a larger than usual dose of wit and theatrics. The audience was very responsive. But let this be a lesson to all of us to inform ourselves fully so we can rehearse properly right from the start.

Grab any opportunity to work with a translator in front of a non-speaking audience. You will learn techniques you didn't know you had. It's challenging because it feels unnatural having big gaps while your sentences are being translated. It's another reason why you really need to rehearse and know your material inside out.

Business pitches

> '*A pitch does not take place in the library of the mind, it takes place in the theatre of the heart.*'
> — Stephen Bayley and Roger Mavity, entrepreneurs

The general rules of rehearsal also apply to business pitches. Run through your material so you are fully prepared, at home or somewhere quiet. It is the time invested in rehearsing that will make that final performance credible. If you want to win, it's essential that you and your team have a practice run-through. Work out exactly where you will all be sitting or standing. Choreograph handovers between presenters, double-check you've got all your materials, and practise every move so it comes together smoothly.

Every member of the team needs to come to the pitch rehearsal having done his or her homework. I was working with a group of professionals who were about to pitch for a significant piece of work. One woman lacked confidence about presenting but she was the most crucial person in the pitch. Her colleagues were used to presenting on a regular basis but she wasn't. She was out of her comfort zone, so I offered to coach her one-on-one to work through her fears. After the actual pitch, the client sent an email with feedback about the performance and this woman was identified as the star performer. Putting in the work meant she'd gone from the bottom of the class to the top!

If you are well rehearsed you will have more of a chance to win the pitch. A part of this is to thoroughly research and find out as much as you can about every single person you are pitching to. Make it your business to know what they respond to. Are they humorous or serious and aloof? What style and tone of delivery will make them notice you and the service or product you are selling?

> '*When we are selling our ideas, the audience must first buy us.*' — Peter Coughter, author and coach

A pitch gone bad

Over the years I have seen teams lose an opportunity to bring in a large contract simply because of not rehearsing well in advance. Leaving a pitch rehearsal to the last minute is fraught with high stress. Cues are missed, lines are fluffed, documents are not ready to satisfaction, the team is disconnected and mistakes are made with technology when we don't rehearse. The client always makes an assumption that your content will be appropriate for their business but the way you present, as a team, is what sometimes ultimately determines the outcome.

It's also important to have a conversation about what you will all wear. You don't want five businessmen turning up in blue-striped shirts. It's important also to debrief whether you win or lose the pitch and always get feedback about what went wrong.

Preparing for questions and answers

I personally think that a question-and-answer panel presentation is easier because you're not alone on the stage, and the focus is not on you for the entire duration — there are other people sharing the stage.

At one of my book launches in London, instead of giving a speech the Master of Ceremonies mixed things up by asking me questions (which I was briefed about in advance and for which I had answers prepared). It made the whole presentation more fun and interactive.

I was coaching a successful businessman for a high-profile and prestigious event. His father was being inducted into the business hall of fame and he was to be asked questions on specific topics about his father: for example, what was it like to start a business in the Depression? Did your father have an entrepreneurial bent? He was beside himself with anxiety and physically felt quite sick for many weeks leading up to this event. We rehearsed in his lounge room for a number of coaching sessions until he felt ready. I took him through breathing exercises and relaxation exercises and we rehearsed the questions over and over. The nerves never went away but on the night he was a star, even though the journalist asking him the questions didn't use any of those we'd rehearsed. He said he had a moment of panic inside but was able to tell the stories because he felt thoroughly prepared.

The rehearsal director

Every business rehearsal needs a director to pull the pitch together and get results. The rehearsal director is the person who gets the ball rolling, cues people in, assigns tasks, and notices when things aren't running as they should. Someone needs to set an appropriate mood in the rehearsal and this is the job of the rehearsal director. In a rehearsal the most important quality that a director can have is to encourage the performers to take risks.

> 'A good director creates an environment which gives the actor the encouragement to fly.' — Kevin McDonald, actor

TIPS ON RUNNING A GREAT REHEARSAL

- **Commit.** Manage your calendar well in advance. Allow for at least four rehearsals.
- **Preparation.** Know your content. Do your research.
- **Appoint a rehearsal director** to take responsibility for running the rehearsal.
- **Attitude.** Bring your positive energy into the rehearsal room.
- **Be open to honest feedback** on delivery as well as on the content.
- **Appoint someone to film** the entire rehearsal and play it back so you can learn from the process.
- **Wear the clothing** you are going to wear for the presentation at a full dress rehearsal and get feedback from someone you trust.
- **Technology.** If using YouTube clips, PowerPoint or video conferencing make sure you rehearse well in advance and check the technology works.
- **Rehearse in front of a small audience.** Invite friends, family and work colleagues.
- **Time your speech** so it becomes a habit.
- **Set up the room.** Have at least one rehearsal in the actual venue if you can. Otherwise set up the room as it will be on the day.
- **Concentrate and focus** throughout the rehearsal and put other commitments out of your mind.

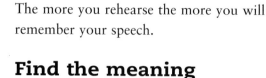

10
Learning the Lines

'Focus on the ideas you're trying to communicate — ideas are easier to memorize than words.' — Theresa Healey, actor

D o you struggle with learning or remembering your speeches? If the answer is yes, then you're not alone. There are ways to help you learn your content. You don't have to read your speeches or rely on PowerPoint or notes to get through. The key is to know and understand your key messages inside out so that even if you lose your notes at the last minute, you can stand up and speak with utter conviction. Know your material and you will give a more convincing performance.

The more you rehearse the more you will remember your speech.

Find the meaning behind the words

You need to understand the meaning behind each paragraph, thought or sentence before you can learn your lines. Understand what you want to communicate, what it is you want to get across, before you even think about learning the material. This is called the subtext of the communication.

> *'At the moment of performance the playwright and the subtext by the actor supply the text.'*
>
> — Constantin Stanislavski, actor and teacher

Constantin Stanislavski's bestseller, *An Actor's Handbook*, was one of my first acting textbooks. Stanislavski says that, 'As soon as people, either actors or musicians, breathe life of their own into the subtext of a piece of writing to be conveyed to an audience, the spiritual well springs, the inner essence is released ... The whole point of any such creation is the underlying subtext. If this were not the case, people would not go to the theatre but sit at home and read the play. We are inclined to forget that the printed play is not a finished piece of work until it is performed on the stage by actors and brought to life by genuine human emotions.'

Make your speech your own and then you will easily remember the material, especially if something goes wrong and the technology breaks down. Find a connection with the material and your emotions. Think of yourself as a storyteller having a conversation with your audience.

If you have written your own speech you are more likely to remember it because you are speaking in your own words. However, speeches are often written by others, such as public relations consultants, freelance writers, press secretaries, journalists or even a talented friend happy to help out. Try to have some input into at least writing the structure of your speech before giving it to a writer to polish.

Ask yourself every time you learn a speech:

- What do I mean here?
- What message do I want to convey?
- How can I learn the material if I don't understand its meaning? This is especially important if the material is technical. If you don't understand what you have written, then it will be difficult to learn and deliver convincingly.

Stage fright

I have a recurring dream where I forget my lines on the stage in a play. I wake feeling humiliated and in a state of panic.

Stage fright is very common when speaking in front of an audience or a crowd of people. It doesn't matter if you work in business, the theatre, politics or education, you are human and sometimes humans forget things.

The more you worry about this the more likely you are to lose your place.

Sometimes in life you get what you think about. Instead of thinking, 'I will forget my words,' try thinking, 'I know my speech backwards.'

Trust your memory. It won't let you down if you have done your preparation and you are focused. Relax, the audience does not always know when you are panic-stricken or even lost for words. They may think you are pausing or creating suspense, or simply reflecting. I remember being mortified one night when I forgot my lines during the performance of a play. I felt exposed and humiliated, and wanted to disappear on the spot. I spoke to friends after that opening night and they didn't even notice when I improvised to cover up the words I'd forgotten.

Be realistic: your memory will fail you at some stage. Be aware that it may happen. If you know your material well enough, you'll be able to think about the points you're trying to communicate, and pick up the flow again. After all, what's the worst thing that can happen? I wish I hadn't spent all those years worrying about forgetting my monologues — my ego was in the way and I was concerned about looking silly. If I'd just relaxed and trusted that I knew my material, my early days of public speaking and performing would have been a lot more enjoyable for both my audience and me.

Techniques for learning your lines

What did you do to study your material before exams at school? How did you become familiar with the material and understand it? There are many ways to learn material and we all learn differently.

Apply your favourite techniques; for example, at school I relied on visuals and imagery to learn. It doesn't matter what you do as long as the outcome is successful for you.

Key messages

What key messages do you want to communicate? If you had to summarize your speech in one sentence, what would it be? A twelve-year-old must be able to understand your presentation.

Here's some jargon to remember — what's your Single Overriding Communication Objective or SOCO? What do you really want to say? In media training SOCO is used a lot to remind clients that they need to know exactly what they want to communicate.

You must work that one message out before you even begin to write your speech. If you cannot do that, then the audience will never know what you are trying to communicate.

Take a large piece of paper or use the whiteboard and write down your main ideas. Next, put them in order of priority. I find it easier to memorize my messages if they are in a logical sequence.

Understand the meaning behind each paragraph. I often ask a client to 'tell me in your own words' when their speech has been written for them by a speechwriter. If you have to deliver the speech in one phrase, what would it sound and look like?

When you are familiar with your material, put your notes aside and rely on key bullet points to jog your memory. Lift your eyes off the page for long periods so they're not darting up and down like a yoyo. Never try to memorize your words and deliver them verbatim unless you are a trained actor.

Beginnings and endings

Do memorize the beginning and ending of your speech. The audience will particularly remember these sections, so it is important to begin and end with conviction and confidence.

You can't make eye contact with your audience if you're looking at your notes or gazing at the carpet. Once you get through the first few minutes you will begin to feel more confident and start to relax. Knowing the beginning of your speech by heart will help you build an immediate rapport with the audience.

Use imagery

It helps to see images in your head — I often open a speech with a vivid story so I can engage the audience. This way I can easily remember the opening and it gives me time to settle in and relax. Stories are much easier to remember than lists of points. The best way to communicate is to say what you see in your mind. In other words, use your imagination to help you remember.

Think of yourself as a storyteller. You use anecdotes in many aspects of your life, especially if you are a parent. When you learn your material you are able to create magic for your audience because they get to experience your personality.

For example, when I am coaching surgeons for their oral exams I ask them to see the operation in their mind as they answer questions as we role-play an interview. This way they tell the story about what procedures they would use rather than rather just listing the facts from memory. This approach also stops them delivering the answer in a monotone.

Write the words down

Another way to learn lines is to write out the main points of the speech again and again. This works for many people I know.

Say it aloud

Read your speech aloud on your own. Walk around the room at home, away from the busy work environment. Study and apply yourself in a relaxing environment or find some time in a quiet room to practise without any distractions.

Get a friend to help

Learn your material with a friend listening to you and prompting you. Your confidence will increase when you receive praise and feedback.

Record yourself

Use a video monitor and camera and tape your performance. The more you play back your performance, the more you are able to sit back and hear the words, hear the subtext and the speech as a whole. As a result you absorb the messages in it. This practice will help you feel more confident.

Mind mapping

Mind mapping is a useful tool for remembering text. The more relaxed you are the more you will assimilate. Many of my clients use this method to learn business material. They use coloured markers instead of the standard pen or pencil, as coloured pictures are easier to hold onto in your mind.

Learning environment

Give yourself the best possible environment in which to learn your speech. Some suggestions include:

- Playing music that helps you to learn, unless you find it distracting.
- Turning off all phones, radios and televisions.
- Opening a window to get some fresh air.
- Sitting in a comfortable chair.
- Having healthy brain food such as nuts to nibble on. Never try to learn when you are hungry.
- Being alone when you are practising so you have no distractions. One of my more conscientious clients always puts aside some 'going over my speech time — no interruptions'. He is always very centred when he speaks to a large audience because he has put in the time required.

Equipment

I sometimes see speakers relying on PowerPoint to read the text of their speech, thinking they don't need to learn their material. This looks unprofessional and unconvincing.

Ask yourself why you are using this technology. If the answer is 'so I can read the words or feel secure with remembering my lines', then you need to spend more time on your preparation and learn your material. It is off-putting and comes across as stilted to see speakers reading their notes with eyes down on the page or on the computer screen. It sends out a message to the audience, saying, 'I don't think enough of you to learn my material,' resulting in a lack of connection with the audience. Appropriate use of PowerPoint in a presentation can be captivating if the speaker is confident but I prefer presentations without technology. It all depends on the audience, the purpose of the speech and the content.

Keep it in perspective

My niece Sarah is a lawyer and has always enjoyed public speaking. We chatted about her most memorable speech.

'One of the most significant public speeches that I presented was when I was at high school and I entered in a Maori speech competition. I spoke for 12 to 15 minutes in fluent Maori to a packed auditorium of approximately 2000 people. It is traditional in Maori speeches not to use notes, therefore I presented the whole speech without notes and I also presented an impromptu speech in Maori after my main speech. Public speaking is difficult at the best of times, speaking publicly in a second language is even more of a challenge and it required weeks of preparation and rehearsing.'

I walked away from this conversation promising never to moan about learning material again. Sarah is part Tongan and has a passion for the Maori culture and language. When we want something badly enough we will remember our material because we will put the effort into our preparation.

TIPS ON LEARNING YOUR LINES

- **Read your speech out loud.** This way you get to listen to your own voice and learn the content.
- **Learning the bullet points** helps you to remember the structure and you can improvise around the key points.
- **Technology has its place.** I have not used tape recorders or dictaphones but have seen many actors memorizing their lines this way or with an MP3 player.
- **Use colour.** I find it useful to use coloured markers to emphasize key points in my notes.
- **Practise difficult words out loud.** If you keep on fluffing a line when you rehearse, practise it out loud. Practise it as a tongue twister. Don't get hung up on it if you stumble.
- **Understand your content thoroughly** so if you forget your lines, you'll be able to find different words.
- **Make it a priority to take time** to learn your presentation.
- **Visualize the beginning and end** of your presentation, and see a road map for how you intend to get there.

11

Transforming Your Fears with Self-Belief

'Success is liking yourself, liking what you do, and liking how you do it.'

— Maya Angelou, author and poet

Most people have fears around public speaking. In my lifetime I have met very few people who are 100 per cent comfortable on a stage speaking to an audience or who are super confident about giving a speech of any kind.

My research shows me that it is the people who practise their speeches and love their work who are the most confident. To be successful in life we have to be disciplined and it will be your love for your work or hobby that will get you back on a road to success. For me, success is about liking who you are in the world. Maya Angelou sums it up so aptly.

Many clients who have come to see me have been reluctantly pushed, and persuaded, because they can see that fear of public speaking is crippling their career opportunities. If you want to grow as a person you must conquer stage fright, and this chapter will give you a few tips to make you feel more confident. It is rewarding to stand before a group of people and inspire them with your stories and ideas knowing you have touched people's lives. We soak up new information and admire people who share their knowledge. Always remember you are unique and you do have something to say.

We certainly aren't born with a fear of public speaking; it's a learned behaviour. Can you remember a time when you were told you were no good at speeches as a child, perhaps when you gave a morning talk or participated in a school debate? Were you laughed at, put down or discouraged from speaking again? Try to think about where your fear of public speaking may stem from.

Experts get nervous too

We see actors, politicians, television presenters and celebrities speaking at functions and think their confidence comes naturally. Many of them have been trained and have a job that requires them to speak in front of a crowd, so they hone their skills on a regular basis. However, even for experts, the nervousness doesn't go away. We never think of experts such as professional actors being afraid of speaking in public.

I have worked with newsreaders and television presenters for over 20 years who tell me they want to improve and feel more confident. I respect these professionals. They are at the top of their game but they still see value in having a coach. Their audience is everyday people, watching from their living room couch. They may never meet their audience but they still commit to lifting their act.

Actor Joel Tobeck, known for his work in the American series *Sons of Anarchy* and the fantasy television series *Hercules*, says, 'I like the sense of freedom when I speak or perform in public. If the audience enjoys my performance, so do I … However, I still feel paralyzed sometimes and ask myself, why am I doing this? Then the theatre takes over and you go on your professional instincts. As long as you trust yourself you won't look a fool. It took me ages to learn this.'

> 'Our deepest fear is not that we are inadequate. Our deepest fear is that we are powerful beyond measure. It is our light, not our darkness, that most frightens us. We ask ourselves, who am I to be brilliant, gorgeous, talented and fabulous? Actually, who are you not to be?

You are a child of God. Your playing small does not serve the world.' — Marianne Williamson, author

The second sentence has resonance with me. 'Our deepest fear is that we are powerful beyond measure.' (Over the years this famous quote has been credited to Nelson Mandela, but he has said several times that these words are from Marianne Williamson and not from him. I became aware of this after attending a speech given by Williamson in London. Collect your favourite quotes to inspire you. Read them the night before your presentation. The power of language is there for you to use to your benefit.)

Witi Ihimaera, who is regarded as one of the most prominent Maori writers alive, and who wrote the acclaimed novel *The Whale Rider*, also feels nervous before speaking in public. He says, 'My mother used to say whenever I was anxious, "What's wrong with you? It's only 15 minutes of the rest of your life." Whenever I face an audience and my knees start to tremble I always think of that and it helps get me through.' Witi's mother's advice is valuable for all of us. We sometimes attach too much meaning to everything we do in life.

Brené Brown, a research professor, author and public speaker, has some great TED talks and has appeared on CNN. I identify with her teachings and work because she talks about courage, compassion and connection, values that are important to me and that can also help you to overcome your fears.

What are your fears?

A fear of public speaking is actually a fear of rejection. When I earned a living from acting I was constantly afraid my directors would say, 'You cannot act.' Of course, they never said that but the fear remained. They would say, 'You can improve,' and tell me what I was doing wrong though.

The pre-course questionnaires that we send out to clients before they work with us have a common theme about fears. The quotes opposite are from senior leadership managers from one company in a response to the question. 'What are your fears when speaking?'

Do you relate to any of the following quotes? Get a pencil and tick off the phrases that you relate to.

- That people will not find me interesting.
- I can be intimidated by high-ranking officials or people working at a higher level role who have much more practice and experience.
- Not being able to find the word I am looking for; having a 'brain freeze'.
- I can sometimes be too passionate and speak too long.
- I don't enjoy being in the spotlight.
- Forgetting what I am going to say.
- Getting off track — all over the show and speaking too quickly.
- Clamming up. Poor reception.
- Making mistakes and how people judge me.
- Not connecting with the audience; I don't get the message across that I am trying to present.
- Giving a presentation where the audience views me as a bad presenter and it was a waste of time.
- That I will lose credibility through poor delivery or lack of subject matter knowledge.
- To accidentally provide inaccurate information due to nerves.
- I expect myself to have the answer to everything.

From all my research and experience of working as a coach, everyone has a universal fear of rejection on some level. This is only my point of view. It's not based on surveys or academic research but even the most experienced business executives that I work with confess to me that they feel uncomfortable and worry about being rejected — whether it be speaking to the media or on a stage. I'm yet to meet the person who is fearless. The reason why presentation coaches are busy is because there is a need.

> *'I am always terrified when I perform or sit down to do a read-through of a new play. I breathe deeply and focus my thoughts. I ask myself, what am I afraid of? I say to myself, you know everything you need to know about what you are about to do.'*
> — Raymond Hawthorne, actor and playwright

The effects of stress on the body and the brain

Understanding how your body and mind react in times of stress will enable you to manage each situation. When we get stage fright and go blank in front of an audience it is because the stress chemicals are affecting our brain. I've had clients tell me they were paralyzed with fear when they delivered their speech. Others have felt nervous and flustered, which is also due to the effect of stress chemicals on the brain.

When you are afraid, stress hormones are released into your body, resulting in a burst of energy that manifests itself as a pounding heart, intensified breathing, memory loss and sweaty palms. When we feel threatened our fight-or-flight reflexes kick in and the body directs all the blood to the brain. That burst of adrenaline before you start speaking is necessary to kick start a great performance.

Strategies — looking after yourself to counteract the effects of stress

Academic Bill Lucas says, 'The brain's efficiency can be reduced to as low as 10 per cent in pressure situations.' He suggests that plenty of water, a good diet, enough sleep, visualization and studying others can help. Stay away from processed food — it is not good for you. If you want more information, read Chapter 14 on health and wellbeing.

Fear of not being good enough — and how to overcome

When I started out as an actor I would sometimes decline television and film auditions because I was terrified of failure. I turned down the opportunity to audition for *Xena: Warrior Princess*. If I'd gone for the audition I possibly would have received a small guest role. Lucy Lawless, who played Xena, was in an acting scene with me in a Raymond Hawthorne master class. She was a joy to work with and I would have enjoyed working on the series with her. I should have trusted myself more.

I used to compare myself to other more talented actors like Lucy. This did not serve me in any way. Working in professional theatre taught me invaluable life lessons about feeling the fear and doing it anyway.

The day I got my first lead in a short film, which won an international award, was the beginning of my accepting every audition. I knew I could do it; I even called my agent after the audition to say, 'I'm going to get this role.' It took a lot of hard work and determination to get to that stage. You can make a decision to change and overcome your fears. No one can do it for you. You have to choose to do it.

The fear might never go away completely but know you are perfectly human! Most of us are nervous when we face a new experience or if we do not know what is going to happen.

According to research by author and presentation coach Lenny Laskowski at the Princeton Language Institute, 'Thorough preparation reduces your fear by 75 per cent.' In his experience, 'Proper breathing techniques can further reduce your fear by 15 per cent, and your mental state accounts for the remaining 10 per cent.' In my own experience, deep breathing helps me to manage my nerves before I speak to a large audience. In every workshop we teach our clients how to breathe correctly so they understand that shallow breathing is not useful.

Step out

Psychologists specialize in the diagnosis and management of stress and many see clients with a phobia of public speaking. I sometimes refer clients who have a phobia of public speaking to clinical physiologists. I also recommend weekly public drama classes or Toastmasters. Once you enrol in a class you will meet others who are like you, reluctant to stand in the spotlight. You will be amazed at the changes you will make.

Improvisation

What is valuable about improvisation is that it requires good listening and teaches people to be flexible and roll with whatever situation comes up. Improvisation takes you out of your comfort zone and you get to experience that it's not so scary. There is no script, no set lines but you start to use your own imagination to create a scene and trust yourself to deliver great content. After all, in everyday life we improvise and make things up on the spot. I took a business client, who was coming to me for presentation skills, to an improvisation class many years ago and he never looked back.

If you live in Chicago go to a workshop or attend classes at The

Second City. I listened to a stimulating radio interview about their work in creativity. They also have a book out called *Yes And*.

EXERCISE

The improvisation exercise 'Yes And' has no script to follow. You work with a partner and affirm each other, building ideas by using the phrase, 'Yes, and'. For example, read the follow conversation:

> Person A: 'It's a beautiful day outside.'
>
> Person B: 'Yes, and outside is so nice we should go for a swim.'
>
> Person A: 'Yes, and swim all the way to the island.'
>
> Person B: 'Yes, and the island of the dolphins is close — let's go there.'

This exercise can be applicable in business too as businesses are always creating ideas from a blank sheet. Actors all over the world are taking their creativity into business to help people to feel more confident.

Toastmasters

Many of my clients around the world belong to a local Toastmasters club and they find it useful. I often suggest to clients that they go to Toastmasters to practise public speaking in a non-threatening environment. The Toastmasters organization has an excellent track record internationally, and it is based on the principle of small groups of people meeting regularly to practise different types of presentations. If you don't have the opportunity to speak in front of an audience in your work or private life, this is the perfect opportunity to hone your presentation skills. Some of my clients have said they very rarely get the opportunity to speak in front of others, so when they do they feel rusty and frightened. Joining a public-speaking club is an excellent way to overcome these fears and to see you are not alone.

Ask for help

In London I taught regular weekly classes for people who suffered from social anxiety. I felt privileged working with people from diverse cultures who came together for two hours a week with one thing in common: a fear of public speaking. It's possible for you to overcome all of your fears with a little help from someone who has been there. A speaking coach or life-skills coach can be a great help. Hundreds of people have signed up for three months of tuition, saying, 'I don't care how much this costs, I can't go on in my life feeling this afraid.' There comes a time with any phobia or limitation when you have to stop using fear as an excuse and take steps to overcome it instead. I remain in touch with some of my clients who went to these classes and they've gone on to do great things in their careers.

Trust your audience

> '*It is your beliefs about the importance of what other people think about you that make the difference. Fear of public speaking has more to do with the fear of being negatively evaluated by other people than anything to do with the act itself.*'— Dr Gwendolyn Smith, clinical psychologist

During my early business career I hated public speaking and only accepted invitations because it was a necessity professionally or rewarding financially. As the founding director of the Performing Arts Centre in New Zealand, I had to be a spokesperson to media and speak at least once a month in front of a business audience, especially when I was seeking sponsorship. I also had to give speeches to large audiences at fundraisers and host big events in the arts. The bottom line was that I was afraid of making a mistake and afraid of looking foolish. In time my fears diminished. It was daunting for me at first speaking in front of business audiences. Gradually, my perception began to change. I started to realize they were just like me; they were human beings supportive of my vision. I was always amazed when someone approached me and congratulated me on my speech.

Change your habits

> '*I gain strength, courage and confidence by every experience in which I must stop and look fear in the face ... I say to myself, I've lived through this and can take*

the next thing that comes along ... We must do the
things we think we cannot do.'
— Eleanor Roosevelt, politician, diplomat and activist

We are often creatures of habit and changing our behaviour doesn't come easily. We like to always sleep on the same side of the bed. Think of all the fears you've overcome in your life. You need to apply the same principles to overcome your fear of public speaking. When I work regularly with clients who are particularly shy or lacking in confidence, I get to see the transformation before my eyes. For example, I have clients who 'um' at the end of every sentence. I'm passionate about deleting these 'ums' because I was an 'ummer'. I have techniques to encourage clients to change their habits and pause at the end of a sentence. In our workshops we use a teaching technique where every time the client says 'um' everybody in the room clicks their fingers. The client then gets so irritated by the interruptions that they break the habit.

Trust yourself

'Everyone can be great.'
— Dr Martin Luther King Jr, civil rights leader

Focus on your strengths. Think of all your achievements in your life. A useful exercise is to write a list of all your strengths. Don't stop until you fill the page. Instead of focusing on your flaws, focus on your strengths.

Values

Values in work and private life are important to my friends and family. It is important to know what your values are. Not only will it help you in writing content for your performance, it will also help with your self-confidence. I surround myself with people whose values are similar to mine.

Learn from previous mistakes

The most successful people never let fear stop them from following their dreams. It is from mistakes and failures that we grow. Without failure we do not learn. The greatest learning comes from that experience when everything went wrong.

> 'Ever tried. Ever failed. No matter. Try again. Fail again.
> Fail better.' — Samuel Beckett, playwright

The power of positive thought

What you think about is what you become. If you think you can, then you're right. If you think you can't, then you're also right.

A number of years ago, the National Scientific Foundation in Virginia estimated that we have between 12,000 and 50,000 thoughts a day depending on how deep thinking we are.

Over the years I have noticed my friends and I obsessing over thoughts relating to the past or the future. It's taken extreme discipline and practice over the years for me to push the delete button every time I have a negative thought. I have to work on it every day, particularly when I go to make a speech.

According to a researcher at the Mayo Clinic in Rochester, 'Being cheerful keeps you going. Optimistic people live about 19 per cent longer than pessimists.' 'It confirmed our common sense belief,' said Toshihiko Maruta, a psychiatrist who was the lead researcher in the project. 'It tells us that mind and body are linked and that attitude has an impact on the final outcome, death.'

To change your state of mind you have to be willing to put in the hard work. Those of you who have given up smoking will know what I'm talking about.

Affirmations

> 'I am the greatest, I said that even before I knew I was.'
> — Muhammad Ali, professional boxer

What is an affirmation? An affirmation is a strong positive statement that something is *already so*. Affirmations are based on the following principles:

- The outcome of your presentation will be a direct result of how you think about it.
- Change your thinking and the outcome of your presentation will change.
- Affirmations help you to change your thinking.

Of course, affirmations can be used in many different circumstances, not just in preparing for a presentation. I often use affirmations in other parts of my life.

Your personal beliefs have a major impact on your performance when you communicate with an audience. I was consumed with negative thoughts the weeks before most opening nights in the theatre or live television shows. What if I fail? What if I'm not good enough? Why am I doing this? I could fill this page with the destructive dialogue that went on in my head. Realizing I needed to find a way to be more constructive with my thinking, I redefined my thoughts after observing successful friends who became my mentors and were living examples of how positive thinking could change a life. The more positive I was the more successful I became.

It's useful to read books or download podcasts or e-books on positive affirmations on the subject that you're interested in. For example, search for affirmations on self-confidence and listen to them on the way to work in your car, on the train, or on the bus. Write them down in a notebook or read them aloud. Sometimes I repeat one silently over and over, especially before a keynote address. Try to be specific. Here are some affirmations you could use before you speak in front of any audience.

- I am present.
- I am a dynamic presenter.
- I am prepared.
- I am excited about giving my best presentation.
- I am an expert in my field.
- I am talented.
- I am going to wow my audience.
- I am confident.

- I am credible and professional.
- I am calm and relaxed.
- I am enough.

Turn the negative into a positive

> *'I get nervous before every single match. It doesn't even have to be a big game — the pressure is always on.'*
> — Serena Williams, professional tennis player

Here are some comments from one of my public-speaking seminars. The participants were asked to write down all their negative thoughts related to public speaking. They were then asked to replace these thoughts with constructive thoughts.

NEGATIVE	POSITIVE
I'm going to make a fool of myself.	I am giving the performance of my life.
Nerves will take over.	I am confident and in control.
I say too many 'ums'.	I am a fluent speaker.
I hate large groups of people.	I am at my best in front of groups.
It's going to be a disaster.	I am well prepared.
I will forget my lines.	I have learned my speech well.

Do you identify with any of these statements? Write down your negative thoughts about public speaking and consciously identify the positive alternative.

Visualize your performance

The *Collins English Dictionary* defines visualization as 'a technique involving focusing on positive mental images in order to achieve a particular goal'. Let your imagination help you in your rehearsals for major speeches or presentations. When you practise, see the venue in your mind, see the audience, and imagine their positive response to your speech. We use visualization often without realizing it. Some people use this tool by painting a mental picture of the end result. Others find it useful to cut out pictures and create a vision board. In our workshops, particularly with athletes, we hear stories about how useful it is to visualize a positive outcome.

> **'Visualization may be the most underutilized success tool that you possess.'** — Jack Canfield, motivational speaker and
> co-author of *Chicken Soup for the Soul*

You can apply this approach to creating a successful outcome for your presentation or speech. Use 'I am' affirmations, as if it's already happening rather than 'I will' which implies the future. Have an open mind. We attract into our lives what we imagine most vividly. I always imagine my audience to be alert, focused, contented and motivated. This makes me feel more confident.

EXERCISE

Get into a relaxed comfortable position, either sitting or lying down. Relax your entire body, closing your eyes. Now imagine yourself at the lectern or in front of your audience. You are speaking with confidence, and know your key messages well. Your audience is excited and they are sitting on the edge of their seats. You finish your speech to warm and genuine applause from a smiling audience. They wait around to spend time with you because they are so inspired by you. You are offered another paid speaking engagement out of this. A successful presentation!

Have you ever used visualization to achieve something you wanted badly? I have often and I am so grateful to the authors, experts and my friends who taught me how to use this technique. It is so easy to become sceptical about anything that is unconventional. Don't knock it until you try it.

Visualization and affirmation guidelines

- Have an open mind. Remove conversations like, 'this won't work' or 'this is hocus-pocus'.
- Phrase affirmations in the present tense, not in the future.

- Define your goal, such as increasing your confidence.
- Create a mental image.
- When you have accepted an invitation to speak, focus on it clearly throughout the day, so that it starts to feel like a reality.
- Think about yourself positively.
- See yourself as a motivational communicator.
- Hear the applause and see yourself receiving fantastic feedback.
- Make your affirmations positive. Affirm what you do want, not what you don't want.
- The shorter and simpler the affirmation, the more effective it will be.

Stopping negative thoughts

'*Every day declare for yourself what you want in life. Declare it as though you have it!*' — Louise L. Hay, author

TIPS ON OVERCOMING FEAR AND BELIEVING IN YOURSELF

- Write down your goals relating to improving your speech or presentation.
- Join a drama or improvisation class.
- Think positively. Stop all self-criticism.
- Practise positive affirmations before every presentation.
- Confide in someone or hire a coach about your fear of public speaking. A problem shared is a problem halved.
- Use visualization techniques.

12
Technology and Social Media

'Technology gives us power, but it does not and cannot tell us how to use that power.' — Jonathan Sacks, rabbi and philosopher

L ove it or hate it technology is here to stay! With the advent of the internet, social networking, mobile technology, and all the apps that accompany them, our lives have changed enormously and will continue to do so in ways that we cannot begin to imagine.

- Forty per cent of the world's population now has an internet connection.
- Nearly 1.4 billion people are active Facebook users.
- Over 300 million photos are uploaded onto Facebook every day.
- Every minute of every day, 300 hours of video is uploaded on YouTube.
- For every 10 minutes spent making international phone calls on every mobile and landline network in the entire world, four minutes are spent on Skype.
- Over 1.75 billion people now use smart phones.
- In 2014 LinkedIn had a worldwide user base of 300 million.

- More people on the planet have access to mobile phones than to toilets, according to a United Nations research report published in March 2013.

The tentacles of technology are evident from Timbuktu to Texas, Toronto, Toowoomba and Tauranga. Even though 'sexy' tech statistics litter the internet, what I know is that there's more need than ever for people to communicate with confidence and presence.

The potential for you to appear on television may not be as high, but it's highly likely you'll need to create a YouTube clip. Increasingly you'll need to look and sound good on an in-house video, present well in an office Skype meeting or know how to pose confidently for a really good photo. The opportunities to 'put yourself out there' have never been more abundant, the competition to be seen and heard is massive. Those who succeed arc those who prepare, plan, practise and stay open to learning and creativity.

In this chapter I explore a range of commonly used technology — new and old — and look at how 'tried and true', seemingly old-fashioned common sense and presentation skills apply more than ever before.

- You may have the technical smarts to put yourself up on Facebook, but if you don't know what makes a good story, how to tell it and make it interesting in 100 words your readers will quickly move on.

- If you can't craft a witty, relevant and topical 140-character sentence, and don't have the savvy to promote yourself, your work or your events, you're unlikely to become a successful Tweeter.

- Yes, you can now shoot video off your phone and upload it online with the click of a button, but what does it look like in the end, and is it likely to be useful or memorable to anyone else?

- You can save time and money by meeting via teleconference, but if the meeting's badly run and staff are not trained to present effectively, it's likely to become a crashing bore that people dread attending.

- And then there's 'death by PowerPoint'.

I date back to fax machines and can remember the luxury of using email for the first time. I can remember trying to sleep with my fax going off in the middle of the night as I kept it on for overseas clients. I also remember carrying a huge 'heavy as a brick' mobile phone, and using a pager to take my calls. I was an early texter and a committed mobile phoner.

Over the years I have seen the best and the worst of technology in my training. I still have to be prodded and poked by friends and colleagues to keep up with the avalanche of new technology flooding the market. Some of my biggest clients have come through my website or LinkedIn, so I know only too well that I need to connect and communicate in a range of new ways.

All this said, I know my strength is in face-to-face communication and presentation whether I'm using technology or not. Nowadays I prefer to stand and speak without props or technology. I see it as a one-woman show where my gift is to be fully present and talk to my audience. I know how powerful this is for me and for others. Someone once described it to me as 'sending a handwritten card rather than an email'.

Technology as an aid

You will still be the 'star turn' whether you use technology or not. Never undervalue the contribution you make; your stories are enough!

Technology should serve your audience and add value to what you have to say. Don't use it as a crutch to hide behind or rely on when you lose your way. You will insult the audience if you read text off the screen, when they can read it perfectly well for themselves.

A 2014 Forbes article said it all for me when it reported that 91 per cent of listeners at business presentations admitted to daydreaming and 39 per cent said they'd fallen asleep in PowerPoint presentations! I still see clients using boring text-heavy PowerPoint with few attractive graphics and visuals in their slides. As the quote goes 'absolute power corrupts and absolute PowerPoint corrupts absolutely'.

Technical rehearsals

Whether you're presenting on Skype, using PowerPoint, video or any other technology, you need to rehearse. Actors are professionals on opening night because they've rehearsed for weeks. A technical rehearsal shouldn't focus on the content; it's about making sure the technology is working properly. Make a point of trialling the technology before you speak. It can be fickle; I had a client who was adamant about using a clip of an old movie in a business presentation. It worked in three rehearsals but on the big day in front of the entire staff, it didn't!

A former client told me recently about an important telephone conference from New Zealand to the United Kingdom where the group were all upside down! Technology can break down, so always have a back-up plan. Don't beat yourself up if it happens but do look at what went wrong and try to prevent it happening again.

When I help clients pitch for work I insist on scheduling rehearsals if PowerPoint is being used. It is a turn-off, sitting in the audience, watching someone fumbling with PowerPoint or other equipment. Once you are familiar with technology it always becomes easier. Knowing in advance that your technology is properly set up, and being comfortable with what you are going to say, are definitely the keys to success.

No assumptions

If you are speaking at a function that you're not coordinating, don't assume the technology you need will be available or compatible with your computer. Tell the organizers exactly what technology you need. Call in advance and set up arrangements for playing your PowerPoint or video. Make sure you have a name and contact number for the resident technician at the venue you're presenting in.

I hire a cameraperson I know and trust to film my presentations. You may want some of your presentations to be used on your website, so make a point of recording your work, even if you pay someone to edit it for you later.

If you're asked to speak, check to see if your presentation is being filmed as you may unwittingly find yourself on someone's website, without being really prepared. In these circumstances you may need to sign a contract. This was the case for me when I spoke to a group of underwriters and brokers for a global insurance company recently.

Have a back-up plan

If your technology fails, you need to be sufficiently comfortable with your material that you can carry on regardless. For example, if you're using PowerPoint, have a copy of your slides and a leave-behind document ready to distribute at the end of your speech; if your PowerPoint fails, your listeners will have the material to take away. Make sure you take a memory stick with the presentation on it, have your power cord just in case your battery fails, and check the wireless internet connection when using Skype.

An audience is forgiving when technology fails, but you need to stay calm and have the confidence that you can find a solution in a short timeframe. Make sure you practise the 'What if it breaks down?' scenario in your rehearsal. Remember that if you have a technician present they are paid to worry about this, not you. Never speak to an audience without having a full technical rehearsal. There is no excuse.

Presenting on Skype

Skype is now an essential tool and has opened up the world of communication to families, friends and the business community. It is not unusual for me to receive an email like this one.

> Hi Maggie,
> I'm speaking at TEDx on Friday. Thinking about all the help you have given me over the years and really missing you incredibly right now.
> This is on the off-chance that you will be around to Skype in the next 24 hours.
> Much love, Jean

My friend and colleague had never spoken at a TEDx event before and was incredibly nervous. I was able to give her 30 minutes of phone coaching before she wrote her speech, send her off with some homework and offered to coach her on Skype the next morning. I prefer coaching face-to-face but like to be accessible, especially when I've trained the person before. A reassuring voice and expertise can make a difference in a short timeframe, and Jean's gratitude and success was my reward.

Wendy Kerr, a leadership coach, conducts a successful business with UK clients from New Zealand using Skype. Without it her business wouldn't exist. Here are her tips for success:

'Think of it as if you're in the same room as the person you're speaking to. You want to be seen as a professional, so pay attention to the lighting, the background behind you, your appearance, and the position of your face on the screen.

'I have invested in high-quality lights to brighten up my image and also ensured my background is professional. Always have a friend Skype you to check lighting, background and the overall impression.

'One more key tip — get to your call early and always check your microphone, camera and speakers. Even if they worked last time it pays to check again. I have been caught out with unexpected equipment failures.

'The other thing I would add is always have a back-up plan if Skype fails, whether a landline, Google hangout or a paid-for online meeting provider.'

There are so many benefits when using Skype. You can communicate with anyone, anywhere at any time. It can save you time, money and resources. You can also have notes in front of you with your messages and achievements highlighted. The key is always to be prepared for things to go wrong. Cover all scenarios. You need to become an expert in crisis management if you want to become a regular Skyper for presentations, interviews and client meetings.

HOW TO USE SKYPE

- Enter the web site http://www.skype.com
- Click on download.
- Click your Skype icon.
- Sign in.
- To invite someone search their Skype username.
- Prepare a headset/microphone to talk.
- Select 'contacts' tab.
- Select contact and click the green icon.
- Click the green call button.

- Wait until it answers.
- Talk for as long as you want.
- Click the video button for camera.
- Click the red button to end.

HOW TO PREPARE FOR SKYPE

- Prepare for a standard interview: preparation, practice, clothing, etc.
- Test your wireless connection: sound, camera, internet speed. Perhaps call a friend to test. Move to another location in an office if needed.
- Check your background. A cluttered background will give the wrong impression.
- Manage potential noise distractions such as barking dogs. Let others in the house know you are giving a Skype presentation so they don't disturb you.
- Review interview details: account name, correct time (including international time differences) and who is calling whom.
- Prepare notes. Write down common scenarios, notes, answers just in case — if you're using a camera, make sure you keep them out of sight.

Autocue and new technology

In 2014, my friend Professor Marylin Waring was the recipient of the prestigious New Zealand Institute of Economic Research Economics Award, in recognition of outstanding contributions to the advancement of economics in New Zealand. It was a big day for the Auckland University of Technology and for Marilyn. What made this occasion even more memorable was that it was the first time I'd witnessed advanced autocue technology in action. When the Vice-Chancellor and others got up to speak it wasn't at all obvious they were reading off an autocue.

This wonderful device sits in front of the speaker and looks like a square piece of glass on a stand. The clear glass is designed to produce a mirror image, so the speaker can see the words clearly while they remain transparent to the audience. This clever design shows how far technology has come and will continue to advance. When I was a young actor doing television commercials I remember finding autocue incredibly difficult because I wasn't practised. If you're using a standard autocue you still need to practise (at least two rehearsals) to get your eyes off the screen and connect with your audience. So, buddy-up with the technical crew, rely on their professionalism and work together to make sure there are no hiccups on the night.

Using social media to enhance your brand

The way you are presented online can significantly affect the way you're perceived personally and professionally. An inappropriate Facebook post or photo can quickly get an online life of its own and have far-reaching consequences for you, your family, team or work colleagues.

The potential for ongoing online harassment and even bullying is also high. This is a public space, so think before you post. The old rule: 'Try not to say anything that would embarrass your mother or your boss' is a good starting point. Be professional and courteous and don't argue online — it's usually a hiding to nowhere!

Finally, remember that what happens online stays online and can still be found years later when you and your nearest and dearest thought you'd moved on.

Look to social media to help you promote yourself, your business, your product or your cause. It's a great way to build your brand, your business, your networks and your confidence. A good example of great social media branding is Helen Clark (administrator of the United Nations Development Programme). Helen completely understands the importance of social media, whether posting on Twitter, Facebook, LinkedIn or Instagram; her photographs are fantastic and interesting, her content is always appropriate and engaging. The whole package allows friends and thousands of followers to keep up with what she's doing, understand the issues she's pursuing and get involved if they want to.

Websites

'Four years ago nobody but nuclear physicists had ever heard of the internet. Today, even my cat, Socks, has his own webpage. I'm amazed at that. I meet kids all the time [who've] been talking to my cat.'
— Bill Clinton, former US president, October 1996

By September 2014, a billion websites had been recorded worldwide. This was expected to stabilize above a billion in 2016. I find it hard to comprehend that in the period I worked in corporate public relations the world went from one website in 1991 to the 1 billion plus we have now.

- The first-ever website (info.cern.ch) was published on 6 August 1991 by British physicist Tim Berners-Lee.
- In 2013 the web grew by more than one third: from about 630 million websites at the start of the year to over 850 million by December 2013 (of which 180 million were active).
- Seventy-five per cent of websites today are not active, but parked domains or similar.

The market is teeming with advice on website creation, design and management. This is well beyond my scope of expertise, especially as there are thousands of people more qualified than I am to give advice on the subject. But what I do know is that your website provides an important platform for you to tell your story, promote yourself and your brand. Here are some things I've found useful:

- Whether you're developing a new site, maintaining an existing one or looking to use your site more effectively, shop around, get good advice and look at the demonstrable results of the company or contractor you're planning to work with.
- Look at why you need a website and what you want it to do.
- Once you're up and running update it regularly and feed it with good content — some experts suggest you spend an hour

a week on this. It's easy to become lazy and forget about it. If you run your own business or freelance, it's even more important because this really is your front door!

- Make sure your website is user-friendly and easily navigated by as many people as possible; it also needs to have a strong connection the rest of your online activities like your Facebook page and Twitter.

- Use colours that mean something to you and make sure you have a design that suits your personality and brand.

- Testimonials, quotes, great photos and recent work are all important. Always think about what your clients or potential clients would want to know, what would reassure them or excite them. A majority of my clients are senior executives who need to feel safe with a coach who has a good track record, so I work hard in this area. I'm blessed to have worked with many high-profile people who are prepared to endorse me. I am very grateful for their support and never underestimate the doors they help me open.

- Pay attention to detail and make sure that any problems on your site are fixed quickly. A client wanting to send out my website details to eight workshop participants called recently to say my website was down. I'd been so busy I hadn't noticed. I also missed seeing an email that funds were due to me.

Hundreds of my clients come through my website because someone has mentioned my name. Take control of your brand. It's never too late to re-invent it or recreate your business online. You don't have to manage your own site or keep your own social media up to date. The most important thing is that if you haven't got the time or skills to do it, you need to make sure someone who cares almost as much as you do does it.

Facebook

Every 60 seconds 510 comments are posted on Facebook, 293,000 people update their status, and a staggering 136,000 photos are uploaded. What this means for most of us at work or in our own businesses is that it's too big to ignore.

I was always a bit shy and hesitant to update Facebook and this has meant I've missed so many great opportunities to post and update my site. For example, a photograph of me and Bill Clinton at a Cure Kids event in Auckland or a photo of me and Ruby Wax speaking at an event in London. I now realize that to sell my books and services I have to make the time to embrace social media and not be embarrassed.

I have a number of friends who choose not to be on Facebook for professional reasons; however, they do have great websites where they conduct a lot of their business. The first thing employers or businesses do when they want to hire you is to check you out on Facebook, so anything you post has the potential to influence how others see you. Pictures of you intoxicated at a weekend party, compromising relationship shots, political sideswipes or online arguments won't serve you well. My nieces and nephews know the Maggie rule: no Facebook photographs at family celebrations unless I see them first!

LinkedIn

LinkedIn is the world's largest professional social network where you can grow your connections, job opportunities and network with professionals in your field. It provides a space for recommendations and testimonials from colleagues as well as an online résumé.

- In 2014, 41 per cent of people using LinkedIn reported 500 plus connections and 15 per cent said they had more than 1000 connections.

- Forty-eight per cent of people who use LinkedIn say they spend more than 2 hours a week on the site.

Before any professional business meeting I go on to LinkedIn to learn about the person I am going to visit. I often take a print out of the LinkedIn résumé to meetings if I want to jolt my memory about specific jobs. It's a quick, easy way to do your research. One of my biggest clients came about through an HR manager tracking me down on LinkedIn when I lived in the United Kingdom. Like Facebook, LinkedIn needs to be updated regularly. I'm the first person to put my hand up and say I don't do it as well as I should, but many of my clients are great role models and have shown me how valuable this resource is.

Videos and YouTube

There are currently 4 million video viewings on YouTube daily. Video is hot property online and appears to be an increasingly attractive medium for viewers, whether it's posted on Facebook, YouTube, Instagram, Vine, your website or any other platform.

It's a great way to tell a story about who you are, what you do and what you care about. Make sure it's short (under 2 minutes), authentic and visually attractive. You can shoot and upload your own video from your smartphone if you have the time, inclination or skills. If you're like me, you can get a professional to do it for you. Most systems come with built-in editing devices, or you can download them off the net. What you do will depend on what you want it for and the end-quality you're setting your sights on. A well-shot and edited video can be put to a number of uses both on and offline, so do your homework and take good advice if this isn't your strong suit.

At the moment I have a promotional video clip, a sample workshop, a sample speech, an interview with a journalist, a series of short clips for Volunteer Service Abroad, and one of someone endorsing my book. I often redirect clients to these clips so they can get a feel for my style and get to know me online before the first meeting.

Twitter

Twitter was launched in 2006 and by 2015 it had 288 million monthly active users and over 100 million daily active users. Although a tweet can only be a maximum of 140 characters it's amazing to see what people share in this very condensed form: links to events, tutorials, academic papers, product reviews and much more.

The landscape of Twitter is changing and growing all the time. In 2009, an analysis of 2000 tweets (from the United States and in English) undertaken by San Antonio-based research company Pear Analytics showed content fell into the following categories:

- Pointless babble — 40 per cent
- Conversational — 38 per cent
- Pass-along value — 9 per cent
- Self-promotion — 6 per cent
- Spam — 4 per cent
- News — 4 per cent

More recently Twitter has been used for a variety of purposes, including major political protests such as the Arab Spring starting in 2010 and continuing through until 2012. It has also been used to put the spotlight on issues such as racism, sexism, civil disobedience, and police shootings. People sometimes use it to break news, the media uses it to promote programmes and shows and increasingly it's being used in emergency management.

The following short etiquette guide for using Twitter may be helpful.

- Have a good biography. If people land on your Twitter profile without knowing who you are they should be able to find out more about you in a few seconds.
- Be selective about who you follow. Only follow those you're interested in.
- Credit your sources. If you share information or retweet a post, make sure you acknowledge where it came from.
- Make use of hashtags. Of the 400 million tweets per day, an average of three are generated from each registered user. Hashags(#) help you search for the information you're looking for in seconds.
- Have a focus for your activities and supply good content, that way you're more likely to benefit from your tweets.
- Engage. Twitter is a two-way street, so engage and interact. Build relationships with other users and create your own network, reply to people who send you tweets or retweet information to you.
- Use the (DM) option to send personal messages to users you follow but don't abuse this system, keep it short, ask for answers or an email address and move the conversation on.

- Don't automate, as it is disrespectful and a waste of time and space.
- Avoid leaking personal information.
- Avoid arguments.

(Source: James Richman, The Community of Digital Professionals)

My friend John Hudson, a New Zealand television presenter and journalist, uses Twitter as part of his work. It helps him advertise and promote the programmes he's working on and he comments on global news regularly.

I used Twitter to promote my workshops in the United Kingdom, advertise services and provide information on specials and deals. It is also provides another opportunity to insert interesting photographs and keep people up to date.

Be careful with the messages you share. Protect yourself and be aware of internet trolls. Promote your business without irritating your followers. Bad twitter etiquette can lose you your followers and tarnish your reputation. We don't need to know what time you got out of bed or what you ate for breakfast. But we do want to know about your opinions, your news and the information you find interesting.

Technology and job interviews

There are positives and negatives to using technology for job interviews. More things can go wrong while using technology, the best thing is to be prepared, know clearly what you want to get out of the interview and feel as if you have some control over the process. Rather than being passive in the interview you need to rehearse more with technology. One of the best things you can do is to role-play with a friend over Skype.

My niece Juliet had her first big job interview on Skype in her flat in London. The connection kept cutting out and quite quickly she realized the coverage in the house wasn't good.

She raced outside in the rain and did quite a long interview in a quiet alcove outside her flat. The next day she received a call saying she had the job organizing large-scale events throughout the United Kingdom.

Architect Simon Clews who is based in Seattle regularly uses online platforms to conduct interviews and meetings. He was employed after using Skype to interview. Here is his story.

'I did my first Skype interview in 2009 when the use of such technology wasn't as wide spread as it is now. I was young and inexperienced in my profession and found myself in a Skype interview for an internship at one of the best architecture firms in America. It was audio only which might have been for the best! Since then I've had experience leading and being part of online meetings and interviews, with colleagues and clients from around the world in many different time zones.

'Thinking back to that original interview, I went through all the standard approaches for any meeting or speech: research, preparation, writing down bullet points, questions, ideas and thoughts. The beauty of being online is you have things in front of you that can't be seen by others. I had lists of questions and answers for things I might be asked. It's important to prepare no matter what form the meeting takes.

'I've been at the firm for a few years now and our use of digital technology in meetings has increased tenfold. I am working on a number of projects in America, and Australia. I've also worked on projects in Korea and Canada; so the need for this technology is always growing.

'Conducting a digital meeting or interview hasn't really changed from 2008 to now. The tools are what change. Have a plan, a structure to the meeting whether it's an agenda (formal capacity) or just notes for yourself. Have things ready, files open on the desktop to share with the group, and watch for conversations going off topic — that is your rudder to steer things back on track. Structure the meeting or conversation to benefit you and your clients, whoever they are.

'Our meeting rooms are all equipped with big TVs and cameras, computers, phones and web phones. We share the computer screen, can hear and see the other person on the TV and can work across countries and time zones. The structure of a meeting never really changes. We are all people, having a conversation and we all have a goal to achieve from it.'

Mina's story

If you're having an interview with a potential future employer overseas, you need to do a lot of homework, research and preparation before you talk to the interviewee. One of my clients, Mina, found this out the hard way.

'I applied for a job in London and was offered an interview via Skype. My experience of the online application process wasn't great, I found it unclear and difficult to use. I liaised with the HR team about the interview process and the manager at the career centre about the role, neither liaised with each other to support my needs as an external client.

'My interview was booked to accommodate the early evening time-table in the Southern Hemisphere. I was told that the schedule was tight and that a timed test would be emailed to me for completion at the end of the interview.

'It felt strange sitting in my lounge at the end of a workday, dressed formally and preparing to present professionally. We tested the Skype connection slightly before the interview and all seemed to be well. The formal interview was with a panel of three people who, while they introduced themselves, failed to "receive" me as an interviewee. There was little scene setting about the context of the job, the interview process or the way questions would be handled.

'Before the interview I was sent a written exercise with questions before the interview and I was told this was my opportunity to talk about what I thought was important about the role. It felt like a dialogue rather than a shared conversation and it was hard to connect, gauge reactions to my answers or create a flow in the interview.

'Midway through, the internet connection failed and I was left

waiting to reconnect. After a few minutes I frantically emailed and phoned to check on the next steps. Finally I received an email suggesting I complete the timed test while waiting to reconnect.

'The delay added to the sense of disconnection I was already experiencing, created additional pressure about time and failed to achieve the purpose of the interview.

'This experience made me review the challenge of conducting important conversations with new people on Skype and the importance of prior preparation including an exchange of expectations. On reflection, a formal presentation with very clear guidelines may have been a better way to start the interview.'

PowerPoint presentations

Used correctly, PowerPoint can significantly enhance a presentation, especially if you're presenting facts and figures. It can provide clarity and impact. The golden rule is to remember you are the star turn, keep it simple, colourful and legible. Judicious use of graphs can help your audience make sense of most financial information.

Correct spelling and grammar are essential. Ask someone to proofread it for you. If you're using visuals make sure your company graphics are up-to-date and used correctly. I well remember a client getting into trouble with his employers because his pop-art visuals were deemed incompatible with the company's brand.

The most common mistake is looking at the screen instead of maintaining eye contact with the audience. Reading a PowerPoint presentation from beginning to end is a sure way to make your audience's eyes glaze over. Learn your material so you don't need to constantly refer to the screen.

Three PowerPoint presentations remain memorable for me: Body Shop founder Anita Roddick talking about her business; Olympic rower Rob Hamill talking about his trans-Atlantic rowing adventure; and mountaineer Peter Hillary talking about one of his trips to the Himalayas. What these speeches had in common was that the three speakers had a powerful story to tell, with or without technology. Their visuals supported their speeches rather than led them.

Tips for using PowerPoint

- Never read the presentation word for word off the screen.
- Keep it simple. No more than one idea per page.
- Check the spelling and grammar.
- Less is best. No more than five words per sentence and no more than five sentences per page. And no more than five slides if you can manage it.
- Use your photos and visuals boldly. One great photo per page is better than three or four small ones.
- Use a font that's easy to read and one that can be seen from the back of the room.
- Make sure your background colour scheme doesn't dominate the look and feel of your overall design.
- Headings should be creative and signpost the presentation.
- Remember your laser pointer and remotes.
- Don't block the screen while you talk.
- Maintain eye contact with your audience throughout the speech.
- If you need to hook up to the internet include this in your rehearsal.
- Graphics should be bold and used wisely. If you source them from the internet, be aware of copyright law; you may need to ask permission.
- Always put your name and contact details on the last slide.

How big should the screen be?

It is incredibly frustrating for the audience not to be able to clearly see the text on a PowerPoint presentation. Technology company Sony recommends the following minimum screen sizes, depending on the number of people you are presenting to.

Audience Size	Screen Size (Feet)	Screen Size (Metres)
Up to 120	8	2.4
120–200	10	3.0
200–300	12	3.6
300–400	14	4.3
400–500	16	4.9
Over 500	20–25	6.1–7.6

Microphones

Your decision to use a microphone will depend on the size of the venue, the number of people you are presenting to and the acoustics. Although you may prefer your natural voice it can be tiring to speak loudly during a long presentation. See if your voice echoes when you're speaking; if the venue has lots of hard surfaces, this is a possibility.

There are three main types of microphone: fixed (usually attached to a lectern), hand-held, and lapel (usually attached to your clothing). If you have a choice, use a lapel microphone as it will give you more freedom of movement.

As well as picking up your words, a microphone can pick up every cough, splutter and sneeze. Don't get hung up about this, but remember to turn off your microphone or hold it away from you if you want to blow your nose or cough!

Do a sound check with someone standing at the end of the room before your speech. If you're tall, don't hunch over the microphone. If you wear a lapel microphone, turn it off when you leave the stage.

Expect technology to break down, because it will. Don't worry about it, go with the flow and be prepared.

I was part of an audience in London listening to a great lecture on communication. Two minutes into the start the microphone went static and the speaker sounded like Donald Duck. What's more, he had invited someone from the audience to contribute, who ended up sounding like Mickey Mouse! We all cracked up laughing. Fortunately the speakers had enough resilience to abandon the faulty technology and quickly execute their Plan B. They projected their voices with power and clarity, and far from the talk being a disaster it was the technical failure that broke the ice and created a more relaxed relationship with their audience.

When I'm a keynote speaker I meet with the technician at least an hour before I speak and do a full technical check. Even when I'm running a workshop at a university or speaking to school students, I spend time with the technician so the event runs smoothly.

Tips on using microphones

- Allow enough time to check the microphone is working and ensure a technician will be there to help if things go wrong. Have a contingency plan in case things don't go to plan.
- Know how to turn the microphone on and off.
- A microphone gives you more volume, but not more enthusiasm. You still need to put expression into your voice.
- Speak above the microphone, not into it. Hold it just under your chin, not in front of your mouth. You're not licking an ice cream.
- When using Skype make sure that your computer microphone is working.
- Take your computer or iPad to your local technology store and test a variety of speakers you can plug into your computer.
- For the best results have a technician present throughout your presentation.

DVD

Playing a DVD during your presentation can be a winner if it is well presented and makes a point. We can get tired of listening to a speaker, especially during a long presentation, and a DVD can provide a change of mood.

If you're going to use a TV screen to play interviews, documentaries or anything visual, hire a large screen with good audio technology. I've frequently sat in large rooms with big audiences where most people either couldn't see the small monitor or couldn't hear the audio due to poor sound quality. I frequently feel frustrated because I know the events would've been sensational if the organizers had spent more money on their technology.

Presenting over the telephone

Speaking in business meetings using a conference phone can be a challenge because the audience you're presenting to isn't in the room. Answer the conference call with enthusiasm and confidence; let your warmth come through. Sound professional and friendly. Organize the venue for the call beforehand so there are no distractions. Listen for non-verbal cues. You need to gauge how your audience is feeling by listening to their responses. Tune in and focus.

A conference phone shouldn't be used to vent anger or express upsets. Tone and manner are everything. Save confidential communication for when you are face to face.

One of my more successful interviews for a business newspaper took place in the PR agency I worked in for eight years in a small room over the phone with the editor. I did an hour preparation and was able to have my material in front of me.

It was satisfying and I was delighted with the outcome when I saw the publication. This may not have happened without my preparation because the editor had a late, last-minute deadline. I was able to feel confident because my key messages were there in front of me.

Tips on presenting on the telephone

- Smile when you speak so you sound positive.
- Stand up or sit tall so your posture is correct and you feel confident and more energized.
- Be in the moment and focus.
- To enable correct breathing, your diaphragm must not be scrunched up.
- Book a private room if you work in open plan.
- Greet the client with warmth.
- Don't read your text messages or emails during your meeting.

Video conferencing

Pay attention to your body language when using video-conferencing technology. Smile, be natural and project confidence. Avoid defensive body language and be energetic with your delivery; your audience can see if you're fidgeting or yawning. Use short, simple, succinct sentences. Be natural. Sit in a comfortable chair (poor posture affects your voice) and use notes if you need them. Some of these tips on the dos and don'ts of video conferencing may be useful:

- Do mute your microphone whenever you're not speaking.

- Do be aware of your video's settings. Check if your microphone is muted before delivering a 2-minute monologue that no one will hear.

- Don't position your camera too low, too high or have it hooked onto a different monitor. Weird camera angles can be very distracting and unflattering. Make sure your camera is eye level and on the monitor you plan to use for the conference.

- Do make sure your room is well lit (side lighting is best). Use natural light from windows or simply turn on the overhead light in the room to brighten up the conference.

- Do wear appropriate clothing. Dress as if you're meeting face to face.

- Do pay attention to art and decorations and create an inviting environment that people want to be part of.

- Do test your microphone by video conferencing your colleague before the meeting. Nothing is worse than trying to share something critical, and not being able to communicate clearly.

- Do, if you're in a group call without video, introduce yourself before you talk. Consider something like, 'Hi it's Jim, I have a question.'

- Don't check or read emails or peruse articles while on the video call. This also includes doing additional work beyond the call. Other participants can tell if you aren't fully focused and present during the video call.

- Do look into the camera when you're talking, instead of looking at yourself talking on the computer screen. It will help others on the call feel like you're 100 per cent engaged and present.

(Source: Bryan Lovgren, Founder of Pinetop Digital Marketing Agency)

Mobile phones

Sadly, mobile phones have taken over our lives. I cannot imagine my life without mine. I used to enjoy the leisurely drive to visit clients listening to classical music. Now I spend the entire journey on speakerphone following up new business calls. I'm weaning myself off the speakerphone so I can focus on safe driving.

Make sure you turn your phone off before you make a speech, give a presentation or attend a meeting. My golden rule is to turn it off the moment I arrive at the venue, as it's very easy to get distracted and forget such a simple thing.

It's inevitable that someone in the audience will forget to turn off their phone, so ask the person introducing you to remind them before you begin speaking. If you're in the audience, make sure your phone is turned off or, if it's an emergency, switch it to vibrate or put it on silent. It's so disrespectful to the speaker to have a phone ring during their presentation, and it can really affect concentration.

I led a two-day presentation workshop at Foxhills, a beautiful country estate outside of London, where the CEO of the telecommunications company employing me asked me to take all the mobile phones from his team at the beginning of each day. The participants were not in the least bit offended and they received their phones back at the end of the day. I'd like to make this standard procedure and would like to see other trainers do likewise.

Using iPads

Many clients prefer an iPad because it's lighter to carry around to a presentation. Be careful when using iPads or tablets to present because it doesn't look very professional if you're scrolling the screen and looking downwards all the time.

Music

If you need to use music from your computer or laptop and you don't have your own speakers, have a practice run-through using the audio in the room. I have music on when people walk into the room but have high-quality small speakers so I don't have to rely on the technology at the venue.

TIPS ON USING TECHNOLOGY EFFECTIVELY

- Ask yourself if it's necessary to use technology in your speech, as it won't be appropriate for all types of speaking engagements.

- Make sure you know how to use the technology if you do decide to use it.

- Have a back-up plan in case the technology doesn't work. Be prepared for a disaster, and arrive early enough to put your back-up plan into action if it's needed.

- Don't expect the technology to help you to be a dynamic and convincing speaker; these attributes have to come from you.

- Set your technology up before your audience arrives. I've seen speakers spend 5 minutes mucking around with equipment while the audience waits. It looks unprofessional and disorganized.

- Technology is there to enhance your communication, not to replace you.

- Skype is wonderful to use but test the wireless connection, run through with a friend via Skype, and check the room and background.

- Use social media to build brand awareness and confidence.

- Educate yourself about social media and be aware of the pitfalls. It's not just about promotion, it's also about engagement and conversations. You can't buy loyal fans and followers.

- Having a social media strategy can grow your business and brand if used correctly. Bad social media can drive away potential clients.

- Unsubscribe yourself if you are irritated with social media.

13
Setting the Stage

'All the world's a stage
And all the men and women merely
players.'— William Shakespeare, *As You Like It*, Act II Scene VII

In a theatre production the set designer has the huge responsibility of creating the perfect set, so what would be your perfect setting? For me, the ambience is essential. You won't always have a choice, but with creative ideas and a creative team you can even dress up an old community hall to look splendid. All you need is a theme and you're ready to go.

The place where you deliver your presentation plays a big part in determining whether your speech will be successful. Your audience will be more open to your messages if you are relaxed. If at all possible become as familiar as you can with the room in which you'll be delivering your speech. If you work in a pleasant environment you'll appreciate how surroundings can affect your morale; it's the same for your audience. Lighting, air-conditioning, room size, decor and sound quality all play an important part in our ability to retain information. We want our audience to enjoy listening to us and to remember our speech or presentation. This means taking the time to create an atmosphere that will allow this to occur — every detail counts.

It's not essential to hold your speech in an upmarket hotel, although this can work well if it suits your content and audience. Think about what type of venue would reinforce the messages you want your audience to remember. I helped a client in London find the perfect hotel to launch her new business. She was leaving the bank that she worked for and venturing out on her own. I took her to one of my favourite haunts called the Haymarket Hotel where I used to work with many clients. She walked into this lavish ballroom and knew it was the perfect setting. What type of venue would help to establish your credibility as a speaker? What kind of impression do you want to make?

Of course, venues can change at the last minute. So, make sure you're prepared to be really flexible. I saw this happen with a team of people who had been rehearsing with me for a number of days. When we turned up for the dress rehearsal, we were informed the presentation was actually to be held on a luxury launch. We had no time for an on-site rehearsal, but we were able to get there early enough to see the stage and make decisions about where the screen was to be placed. If you're familiar with the important points of setting up a room, you'll know what to focus on if your preparation time is cut short.

Venue organizers aren't mind-readers

Always provide your venue organizer or conference logistics manager with a comprehensive brief, setting out your requirements. Email clear instructions about the size of the room, technology required, projected start times and breaks, food and beverage requirements and all ancillary equipment. Then double-check by phone to see if those instructions have arrived. Make no assumptions. Are there any special needs, such as wheelchair access for a disabled member of the audience? Check, check, check and then check again.

Get a name! Should you need to go over the instructions again, it helps to know whom you spoke with last time. When preparing for my workshops I deal with one event manager and always go and see the venue well in advance. I have often ended up making a request to change rooms because it is too small, not soundproof enough, has a boardroom table that can't be moved or no natural light.

Ask questions

You or your support staff should ask the appropriate person as many questions as you can think of. This may seem obvious, but if you run through the checklist later in this chapter you have a good chance of uncovering any hiccups before the day of your speech. Check and double-check that the arrangements are to your satisfaction.

On one occasion I assumed that the organizers of a function I was speaking at would have made a hotel reservation for me as the presentation was out of town. Unfortunately the hotel had made the reservation for the following night instead, and as luck would have it, all other hotels in the city were full. I was upgraded to the grand suite — after some hard words — and I was able to practise my presentation in a luxury apartment. It was sorted out eventually, but it made my preparation for the speech more stressful than it needed to be.

What do you need to check?

A welcoming environment

Would you want to spend time in the designated room if you were a member of the audience? Does the room need fresh flowers? A good tidy up? Some welcoming touches such as a person to show people to their seats? Classical music or some soothing, feel-good jazz?

Think about whether the environment reflects your business brand. Do the furnishings send out an appropriate message? Presenting in a shabby room will distract from your credibility no matter how strong your message. Also think about the size of your room. The first question I get asked is, 'What size room do you want?' and my answer is always, 'Large!' My presentations often involve interaction, so it's really important for me to have space. When I'm giving a presentation in another country I arrive a couple of days early so I can see the venue the moment I step off the plane.

Have a look at the room at least a day before your presentation. If you need to dress the set, then do it. Tell your organizers and technical crew where you need everything or set it up yourself.

I was giving a speech about networking and I had the choice of three rooms. I chose the room with the most natural light, large windows, and glass doors going out on to a balcony. There was tasteful art on the walls and the view of the trees was lovely. If you build a relationship early enough with the event manager you often have the luxury of choosing your room.

Lighting

If you have the choice, deliver your presentation in natural light. Fluorescent light can be a strain on your eyes and sometimes makes a buzzing noise, making the speaker difficult to hear. If you don't have a choice about presenting under fluorescent lights, be empathetic with tired audiences and make allowances for breaks if necessary.

A spotlight directly overhead can cast a shadow under your brow. For major presentations a pair of spotlights (one either side, tilting down at 45 degrees) will make you look friendly and approachable. If you're going to move around the stage, you'll need a 'stage wash', which lights the entire stage. You can hire a lighting technician to advise on appropriate lighting and to provide the necessary equipment — don't feel you have to arrange it all yourself.

Temperature

Temperature is critical to the success of your presentation. There is nothing worse than sitting through a speech when you are sweltering hot or freezing cold. Check the temperature an hour before the audience arrives and communicate any concerns to the staff.

Air-conditioning is not easy to get right but the last thing you need your audience to do is to doze off because it's hot and stuffy. A large audience will warm up the room, so it's better for it to be on the cool side to start with. Somebody in your audience will always let the organizers know if it's too cold. Think carefully about your clothing so you don't get too hot while presenting.

Seating

Ask the staff to remove empty chairs before you start speaking, if this can be done discreetly. Empty chairs remind you and your audience you were expecting more people than have shown up.

Consider the level of audience interaction you would like when choosing your seating arrangement. Usually I like to encourage as much audience participation as possible by removing tables and sitting people in a circle. You don't always have a choice if you are giving a presentation around a client's boardroom table; if this is important, you may like to invite the client to your premises instead.

The size of your audience will determine which seating arrangement you choose. If you're using screens or tables, think about where you want them to go. I prefer a U-shape for audiences of 25 or less, where the seats are arranged in a large circle with a small gap for me at the top. This allows me to maintain eye contact with everyone. Circles and semicircles work because they feel inclusive and informal. For a larger group my preference is a classroom style. Of course, you may not have an option; the majority of my speeches are on a platform with a microphone to a larger audience of 100 or more, where theatre-style seating is the only practical seating arrangement.

SEATING ARRANGEMENTS

Semi-circle/U-shape

For up to ten people, this seating arrangement allows you to have eye contact with everyone in the group and because it feels intimate your audience will be more inclined to ask questions and participate. I prefer not to have a table between me and the audience if possible. If you are presenting at a brainstorming session, a full circle may feel more appropriate.

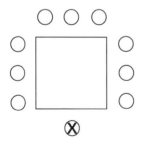

Boardroom

A presentation to a small group around a boardroom table can be useful if your audience needs a surface to write on or if coffee and tea are served during the presentation. Props like flip charts can be useful in this instance. The audience should not sit on the same side of the table as the speaker.

Theatre style

If you're presenting to a large number of people, theatre-style seating is probably the only option you'll have. Remember to place the chairs so each person is looking 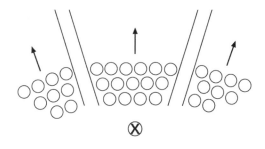 between the two people in front rather than at the back of someone's head. It can be useful to avoid arranging the seating with a centre aisle if you think you'll be distracted by the gap in the middle of the room.

Technology

If you are relying on the venue organizer to provide computer equipment, make sure you have a run-through before the day of the event. I have often sat in an audience feeling frustrated for the speaker because the laptop has been set up on the wrong table or on the wrong side of the room. I've seen many speakers who constantly turn their heads to look at the screen behind them, instead of referring to the bullet points on the laptop's display in front of them. Your microphone is an important piece of technology — even if you prefer not to use one it may pay to have one available just in case you find yourself competing with a road drill or a noisy grader outside while speaking. If you want more information on using technology, go to Chapter 12 on using technology in your presentation.

Music

Well-chosen music builds atmosphere prior to an event or conference, but you must pick the right music for the event. Consider your audience and your subject material when deciding what type of music would be appropriate. Ask other people for their opinion about your music selection. Instrumental music is a safer choice as music with lyrics runs the risk of distracting your audience. Most hotels have an excellent selection of music available for use. If you have clear requirements or set ideas, make sure you communicate this to your contact person at the venue. Fading the music tells your audience that the presentation is going to start. I often play upbeat music 15 minutes prior to my speech and I really notice that as people walk through the door, they perk up.

Handouts and props

You may like to provide the venue with a copy of any handouts you are planning to distribute at the end of your speech, in case you accidentally leave them behind at the last minute. If you are presenting at a conference, there will probably be a date by which you have to provide all your hand-out materials to the conference organizer. Leave yourself enough time to double-check that you have any props you need for your presentation.

Overseas engagements

When I travel to give a speech I always carry everything I might need for the performance in my cabin luggage. I was caught out once when I arrived in New York City minus my bags. I had the casual clothes on my back and nothing else. Fortunately I was staying with a friend and I was able to borrow a blouse and raced down to Macy's in the morning and bought an entire outfit in an hour — paid for by the airline. A client had a similar experience, where everything she needed was in her cabin luggage, except for her shoes. When her bags failed to arrive in Washington DC she had to go shoe shopping, instead of using the rehearsal time to prepare for the speech.

Your venue checklist

- Where is the venue?
- Who is responsible for setting up the room?
- What are their contact details?
- Will they be in the room while you are speaking?
- What date and time is the speech?
- What time will the audience start arriving?
- Where will the audience gather before the presentation?
- Is your accommodation booked (if out of town)?
- How are you getting to the venue? Airfares or taxi fares?

If using your own car, is there parking?

- What equipment will you be bringing? Laptop computer, handouts, music?
- Floppy disc or CD with your presentation hard copy of your speech?
- What equipment do you need the venue to provide?
  - laptop
  - iPod
  - iPad
  - screen
  - microphone
  - lectern
  - music
  - electronic board
  - whiteboard
  - flipchart paper
  - coloured pens (that work)
  - pads and pencils (at back of room or on seats).
- What technical support do you need? Lighting technician, sound engineer? Will they be available for a rehearsal?
- What room will you be speaking in? How big is it?
- What is the seating arrangement?
- Can the audience see you from any seat? Will any plants/ flowers be provided? Can the room be darkened if necessary?
- How is the room's air-conditioning controlled? Is there sufficient natural light?
- Where are the power connections?
- What are the acoustics like?
- Will you need a roaming microphone for people at the back of the room to hear you?
- Can you hear noise from other conference rooms in the building from inside your room?
- Is there adequate access for disabled members of the audience?

- Will food and drink be provided as part of the function? Are there any special dietary requirements?

- Will there be a glass of water for you during the speech? Is there water for the audience?

- What time will the breaks be, if any? Where are the bathrooms?

TIPS ON SETTING UP THE ROOM

- **Communicate** what you need to your event organizers.

- **Go and see the room** well in advance. Arrive early enough to do something about it if it's not right.

- **Let the organizers know** well in advance if you want a lapel microphone, hand-held microphone or a microphone attached to the lectern.

- **Do a microphone check,** including checking the height so you are speaking across it, not hunching into it or over it.

- **Do you have everything you need** such as USB stick, laptops, slides, handouts?

- **Remember to have a copy of your notes.** Don't forget your reading glasses if you need them.

- **Make sure you have a glass of water handy** in case you need it.

- **Be clear** about how you would like the room to be set up. It is your presentation.

- **Build a relationship with your technical crew,** as they are the ones who will look after you.

14
Health and Wellbeing

'Let food be thy medicine, and medicine be thy food.'— Hippocrates

How does your health impact your public-speaking ability? Your health impacts every area of your life. When you're in top shape you can use your energy to make your presentation sparkle.

Sometimes poor health is a short-term occurrence, such as when we're exhausted after a sleepless night or have jet lag or even a shocking hangover. I have often given a speech on a few hours' sleep because the hotel I was staying in was noisy. The challenge is to become energized and focused before delivering the speech.

Longer-term health issues take more work to clear up, but I encourage you to address any problems you may have in order to focus properly on your presentation. If your health issues are outside your control, still take responsibility for living as healthily as possible in order to successfully manage your condition.

Managing stress

Your personal life impacts your professional life. You cannot give a lively, convincing speech if you feel as if your personal life is out of control. In the past I've often communicated with human-resource managers to request time off for clients facing burnout, and to set up support structures to help people realize they must rest and take responsibility for their health. When people are at the point of exhaustion they are sometimes unable to recognize the signs of extreme stress or burnout.

> *'Only intimacy with the self will bring about healing.'*
> — Deepak Chopra, author and public speaker

The Burnout Test

Clive Littin, counsellor and coach, has the following test for assessing how close you are to burnout. Score yourself from 0 to 5 for each question, with 0 being a definite no and 5 being a definite yes.

- Do you tire easily?
- Is joy elusive in your life?
- Do your friends say, 'You don't look well'?
- Are you becoming increasingly cynical, negative, disenchanted?
- Are you invaded by a sadness you can't explain?
- Are you forgetting things like appointments and deadlines?
- Are you increasingly irritable, short-tempered, disappointed in the people around you?
- Are you too busy to do even routine things like making your bed, phone calls, sending Christmas cards?
- Are you seeing close friends and family less often?
- Are you suffering from aches, pains, headaches, a lingering cold?
- Do you feel restless, disoriented when your day is over?
- Do you have little to say?
- Is sex more trouble than it's worth?
- Are you unable to laugh at a joke about yourself?
- Do you seem to be working harder and getting less done?

SCORE:

15–25	You're fine
26–35	Watch out
36–50	You're a burnout candidate
51–65	Burnout
65 +	You're in danger

We all need some stress to perform, as it gets the adrenaline going. However, stress levels become unhealthy when they are out of control. When I make a speech in the middle of the day I organize my schedule around it so I am relaxed and focused. I always go home, shower and change if I have a major presentation after work so I feel fresh. Sometimes I make a note in my diary to go for a short walk several hours before my speech.

It's well known that stress contributes to any illness and increases the symptoms. Being fully prepared before a presentation will help to reduce stress. Increased blood pressure will not help you when you need to feel calm and in control in front of an audience.

Dr Susan Gee, research fellow at Victoria University's School of Psychology, says, 'The way an individual handles a potential crisis plays a part [in stress management]. One person might see stress as a challenge, but someone else may say, "It's too much, I can't deal with that".' Choose not to let the stress of your presentation affect your life. Chapter 11 discusses changing beliefs and using visualization and affirmations to create positive thoughts about public speaking. My personal philosophy is not to view a crisis or stress experience as something bad. Instead, I see it as healthy change or transition. All your experiences are valuable material for your presentations and are nothing to be ashamed of. I have more to contribute because of my failures and weaknesses. Ask yourself, 'Why am I finding this situation stressful, and what strategies can I put in place to ensure it doesn't happen again?'

Medication

If you are prescribed medication for anxiety and stress, work with your doctor so you are monitored.

It can be helpful to research holistic ways to overcome this problem.

One client became so addicted to relaxant drugs she felt she couldn't give a presentation without them. It was her goal to present without medication. She now speaks in front of large audiences drug free. We worked together on her fears and followed a more holistic path.

Headaches

Have you ever had a headache before speaking in public? According to Annemarie Colbin, author of *Food and Healing*, headaches are caused by:

- expansion of the blood vessels in the head (vascular headaches); or
- tension or strain in the muscles in the neck, scalp, or face (tension headaches).

She goes on to say that vascular or 'expansion' headaches are usually the result of:

- too much liquid of any kind, including fruit juice
- alcohol
- ice cream and other cold and highly sugared foods.

Tension or 'contraction' headaches are usually the result of:

- tension and overwork
- heat
- meats and salty foods (especially on an empty stomach)
- lack of food and/or fluids
- excess mental concentration or physical activity in addition to the above.

If you have a headache, consider whether any of the above could be the underlying cause and put strategies in place to prevent the situation from happening again.

Ten commandments for reducing stress

A friend gave me these Ten Commandments many years ago. They were written by Hilary Langford, Founding Director and Principal Consultant, Oliver & Langford. They are a lot of fun!

1. Thou shalt not be perfect nor even try to be.
2. Thou shalt not try to be all things to all people.
3. Thou shalt leave things undone that ought to be undone.
4. Thou shalt not spread thyself too thin.
5. Thou shalt learn to say 'No'.
6. Thou shalt schedule time for thyself and thy supportive network.
7. Thou shalt switch off and do nothing regularly.
8. Thou shalt be boring, untidy, inelegant and unattractive at times.
9. Thou shalt not even feel guilty.
10. Especially, thou shalt not be thine own worst enemy, but be thy best friend.

Look for balance

Finding time to do all the things you want to do is tough. When one area of your life starts to affect the quality of other areas, it might be time to do some rebalancing of priorities. Often, when life gets too frantic, health is one area that starts to suffer because we don't place enough importance on it until we don't have it anymore. Achieving a balanced life takes planning and commitment — simply saying 'I should work less and exercise more' won't work unless you put a plan in place to achieve your goal.

Psychologist Hank van Bilsen says, 'The best protection is a balanced lifestyle.' He suggests a 'reasonably pleasant job' that you don't invest too many hours in, good friends, interests in sports, academic and spiritual things, and enjoying being on your own.

One of my best friends died in her early thirties from breast cancer. She worked in a demanding profession enduring long hours and was also a solo parent. She was always telling me how she wanted to cut down her hours and enjoy life more. Her death woke me up and made me look at my workaholic habits. It made me see that I wasn't having enough fun or setting aside relaxation time. She knew she had a lump in her breast for years but ignored it for a long time. She hated her job but continued with it. Her death made me realise that only I could make myself set aside time to relax and do the things I really wanted to do away from work. Life is not a dress rehearsal.

Medical conditions

Performing requires you to be alert and focused and to look lively and well. I was diagnosed with endometriosis in my early twenties. I had never heard of it — I couldn't even pronounce the word. Many of you reading this chapter will perhaps have a secret medical condition that no one in your workplace knows about. Many years of presenting before an audience when I was ill has taught me to manage my health and my life so I can continue to perform effectively. I initially chose not to discuss my condition with anyone apart from family and friends. However, I revealed the information in one media interview, which changed my mind about speaking out in the workplace and sharing my story in speeches, especially to women.

When I was very ill with the disease the audience never knew otherwise. I have my acting career to thank for that. I would often collapse when I got home, wondering how I was ever going to get out of bed the next day and perform. I have studied nutrition, relaxation techniques, neurolinguistic programming and other helpful techniques that have taught me to manage my health carefully. My personal circumstances influenced me to include this chapter in this book.

I recommend reading *It's a Great Life When You're Well* by Eileen Evans, a registered naturopath. She is a great example of what happens when you live a well-balanced life. In her seventies she still glows with good health. She was presented with a lifetime-achievement award from the natural health industry for dedication to public education. There is a place for prescription drugs, but I highly recommend a straightforward natural health management plan to build your immune system and get you on to a more natural road.

> *'We are far more than our bodies and personalities. The inner spirit is always beautiful and loveable, no matter how our outer appearance may change.'*
> — Louise L. Hay, author

Strategies for coping with illness

A dear friend, Katarina De Nave, had a long battle with leukaemia. She chose to retain her high-profile job in Australia while battling her illness. I admired her attitude, which was always positive. She spoke in public and chaired meetings regularly. Her strategies for dealing with illness were to 'schedule meetings accordingly, take naps, splash water on your face or take a walk'. She advised those living with illness 'not to be hung up on whether you are going to live or die. Get rid of all negativity, including negative people in your life. Get rid of things in your house you do not want. Everyone manages things differently — do what works for you.'

Food and body image

> *'It's not about dieting — it's about changing your life.'*
> — Oprah Winfrey

So many clients complain about their weight when they view their presentation rehearsals. Focusing on your weight gets in the way of a successful presentation and affects your confidence. It's more about looking smart, clean and tidy. Looking professional is what matters.

Working with a client who lost a great deal of weight during the course of a year was an inspiring experience. When I was first introduced to her she was quite large and had very little self-esteem. She decided to embark on a confidence-building journey, losing weight and overcoming her fear of speaking in public. As a result, her life has taken off! When we started working together she wore baggy clothes that were two sizes too big. She now looks elegant, attractive and professional.

Healthy eating

Working with clients to develop a nutritious eating plan has become an important part of my work. I am amazed at the number of people who tell me they don't eat regular meals throughout the day. It is not unusual for me to hear people say, 'I'm too busy to eat.' I used to be one of those busy people who went five hours without food or water and wondered why I was shaking every time I made a speech or led a training session.

Eat lightly, and every three hours, to keep your sugar levels even. Eating well and often has changed my life. I have more energy because I monitor my eating habits. I now eat for fuel.

Breakfast — eat it!

For many years I lived on coffee for breakfast. I had to learn the hard way not to skip the most important meal of the day. Your body needs looking after, and eating breakfast, particularly when you are about to give a speech or run an important meeting, is crucial. Eat breakfast even if you aren't hungry. You need the energy to keep you going.

I have seen many chief executives over the years catching early planes, eating high-fat processed plane food and drinking six cups of coffee a day. It's the easy solution, but it's not healthy. When I need to be on an early flight, I wake half an hour earlier than I need to and eat my standard sugar-free muesli with blueberries, yoghurt and fruit before the taxi arrives. I now arrive for my first meeting feeling lighter and more energetic.

Alcohol

Never drink alcohol before speaking in public; even a glass can result in you slurring or prevent you from performing to your best ability.

Eileen Evans says that alcohol can, both directly and indirectly, cause many illnesses that have been associated with nutritional deficiencies. She goes on to say that experimental studies have shown that 81 per cent of chronic alcoholics, when treated with a well-balanced diet plus supplements, were still sober after six months. Only 38 per cent of alcoholics were still sober after six months when treated with a standard hospital diet.

If you drink alcohol, drink extra water to remain hydrated. Have a few alcohol-free nights per week and remember that alcohol is a depressant, so if you have a speech coming up refrain from drinking the night before. Plan to abstain from drinking for at least a week each month.

Keep a diary for six months

Start observing and writing down everything you eat. This sounds obsessive but it is one way to help clean up your life. A strict naturopath gave me this exercise to kick start a healthy lifestyle. I kept a record for a year and eventually realized the link between the type of food I was eating and my energy levels. I am so grateful to him for helping me to become aware of what I eat.

Exercise

> *'Those who think that they have no time for bodily exercise will sooner or later have to find time for illness.'*
> — The Earl of Derby

Exercise is essential to your mental and physical wellbeing. Find an aerobic activity you love and do it regularly. Thirty minutes of reasonably vigorous exercise four to five times a week will reward you with lower stress levels, a healthier heart, better sleep, more stamina, improved concentration levels ... the list goes on. You simply can't afford not to make exercise a priority in your life.

If you are starting to exercise for the first time or if it's been some time since you last exercised, take it slowly and get a medical check-up before you start an exercise programme. Focus on developing an exercise habit you'll be able to maintain, rather than pushing yourself too hard and then giving up.

Relaxation

> *'So few of us know how to relax. We have come to believe it is necessary to go at 100 per cent all of the time.'* — Dr Sven Hansen, medical practitioner

Recharging at low-cost health retreats has become an important part of my wellbeing regime. When I return from time spent at a health retreat, I am calmer, fitter, happier and ready to get back into my work with more energy. I feel energized after eating only 'clean food' (no meat, salt, dairy, preservatives, coffee, tea or wine) and doing regular exercise.

Attending a health spa is something I do as a result of making a decision to have better strategies in place to manage my health. I realized I was not always as disciplined about looking after my needs as I thought I was. My promise to myself now is to attend a health retreat at least once a year for the rest of my days. I realize the importance of rest and rejuvenation for my productivity and creativity as well as my health and peace of mind. I am of no use to my friends, clients or audience when I am stressed.

You can also implement strategies in your daily life to help you relax and prepare for the day ahead. A high-flying CEO who travels all around the world always manages to meditate before work. She has a demanding role heading up an NGO and finds that meditation helps her to be calm and ready for the day.

There are many forms of relaxation practices. Find one that suits you and incorporate it into your daily life. Investigate yoga, pilates, Tai Chi, the Feldenkrais method, the Alexander Technique, holistic massage or Hellerwork.

When I am tutoring one-on-one I will often get the client to participate in a theatre-based improvisation exercise with me to relax the body and mind. Inevitably they will end up laughing because they feel silly. What makes you laugh? Who makes you laugh? I realise I have surrounded myself with people in my life who lighten me up when I get too serious and worried about giving a speech. Call a friend or colleague who makes you laugh if you feel yourself getting stressed before a presentation. Laughter exercises your throat, stomach, face and diaphragm, stabilizes your blood pressure and strengthens your immune system. It also releases tension and stress.

Connect with nature

Nature heals you and makes you feel better about life. Take a walk before you speak, even if it's just for 5 minutes. Walk to the venue or have a power walk that morning in a park or on a beach. Walking in the fresh air gets your problems into perspective. Wherever I am, walking is my way of relaxing. My exercise clothing is always in my bag when I am out of town for a speaking assignment.

Ask for help

Enlist support when you need it. People will say no if they can't support you. People often refuse to ask for help because they fear rejection, don't want to be seen as weak or a burden, or simply feel they should be able to carry on without support. Get rid of all the 'shoulds' in your language. Some of the best speeches I have given have been as a result of asking for help.

TIPS ON MANAGING YOUR HEALTH

- Drink water or a soothing herbal tea before you speak. Avoid coffee and alcohol before any presentation.

- Always have filtered water with you when you speak and sip it when your mouth feels dry.

- Eat a light, healthy meal at least one hour before your presentation, allowing time for digestion and to give you energy.

- Eat slowly to aid correct digestion. Take time to chew your food.

- Carry healthy snacks such as almonds, muesli bars or fruit so you have energy; your mind needs brain food to aid concentration.

- Speak to a naturopath about Bach flowers, rescue remedy or your local health-food shop about 'mimulus remedy' for stage fright.

- Have a massage the evening before your major presentation. Massages can release anxiety and tension, and will improve sleep.

- Practise some yoga or meditation on the morning prior to your speech or include them in your warm-up routine.

- Go to bed early the night before. A good night's sleep will help you to concentrate more effectively during your presentation.

- Avoid rushing to your speaking venue or meeting. Take time out to be calm. Time management is the key.

- Avoid conflicts or upsets before you see your audience. Clear up any conflict with family, friends or colleagues before you address your audience, or simply be willing to park it to one side and forget it during the presentation.

- Find something to smile about. Laughter before a speech will relax you because it releases endorphins. Five minutes smiling or laughing is all it takes.

15
Clothing Has a Language

'Fashion is very important. It is life-enhancing and, like everything that gives pleasure, it is worth doing well.'

— Vivienne Westwood, fashion designer

Not everyone might agree with Vivienne Westwood's words — we interpret quotes differently depending on our values, cultural background and upbringing — but for me, this quote means that fashion is exciting and gives me the opportunity to express myself on any different day. Westwood is my favourite British designer and I enjoy wearing her clothes because they match my personality. I'm not conventional and neither are her clothes. However, saying that, I also have conservative garments in my wardrobe for when I need them. Clothing has a purpose other than expressing our personality. In the theatre we played different characters, so I sometimes think of my business suits as my costumes.

This chapter is included to give you some ideas about what to wear when you give a presentation. It's also intended to reinforce the message that preparing well in advance will add to your confidence when you present.

Although I am personally interested in fashion you don't have to be in order to make an impact in your professional or public life. But the practical reality is that your style and how you present yourself will shape your image in the eyes of others.

'I dress for the image. Not for myself, not for the public, not for fashion, not for men.' — Marlene Dietrich, actor

Dietrich's acute awareness of shaping her image through her choice of wardrobe is as relevant today as it was half a century ago. According to a recent Harvard University study, we have only 5 seconds to make a good impression. If that first impression is bad, it takes eight subsequent positive encounters to change that person's negative opinion of you.

'You don't get a second chance to make a first impression,' says James Uleman PhD, a psychology professor at New York University and researcher on impression management.

Part of my work with clients is to help them create an image that reflects their tastes and personality and boosts their confidence. I take them shopping for photoshoots, media interviews, presentations and business events. My advice to them is to dress according to the job and plan in advance to avoid stress and anxiety, which can impact performance. It's important to research the dress code before you speak at a function. Dress smartly, tidily and professionally. You will be judged on your appearance.

Just remember, clothing is not about wealth. It doesn't matter what you earn or whether you are a chief executive or student — you can always present yourself well. Secondhand shops are abundant all over the world and you can buy a designer skirt for next to nothing. There is no excuse.

'Elegance is a question of personality, more then one's clothing.' — Jean-Paul Gaultier, fashion designer

Your brand

A personal brand is a phrase used to describe who you are as a person and what distinguishes you from others. It requires you to actively package and market yourself and your talents. Clothing plays an important part in shaping your personal brand. A career defining moment for me was the day I was asked to work with Helen Clark who was then the leader of the Labour Party in New Zealand. She went on to become the country's prime minister and since 2009 has held the third-highest position at the United Nations. Initially, New Zealand media focused negatively on her image — more concerned with how she looked and spoke than her key messages.

According to Brian Edwards, who wrote *Helen: Portrait of a Prime Minister,* 'To her, substance was more important than style and she objected to the idea that how a politician looked or sounded should be of prime importance to the electorate. She was resistant to the idea of being "made over". She was her own person and wished to remain so.'

What used to irritate me — and still does — is the double standard that exists for men and women. During Helen's time in parliament, the media never paid attention to any of the male senior politicians' 'personal brands', image or clothing. I came onboard as one of her media advisors because the constant barrage of negative attention was distracting from who she really was: an accomplished, gifted and highly intelligent woman with enormous integrity. We needed to stop the commentary on her look and image and re-focus it on her competency and character.

Even a top New Zealand women's magazine, which is now defunct, called *Style*, refused to have Helen on the front cover. I fought for it and won. However, it took a lot of convincing. Helen wore a satin gown and cropped jacket designed especially for the shoot by a local designer, Liz Mitchell. She would never have picked this garment herself, but she looked elegant and classic. The feedback was overwhelmingly positive.

Once she was prime minister, Helen saw the importance of image and personal branding. In Brian Edwards's chapter, 'Phoenix from the Ashes', he asked Helen, 'Have you formed any conclusions on the importance of image?' Helen responded with, 'Very important. But you can't do it on image alone. It has got to be style and substance. One without the other won't work. I had an abundance of substance, but I didn't have the style. However, it is easier to do something about that than have an abundance of style and not the substance. You'll never plug that gap.'

Job interviews

Have you ever struggled with knowing what you should wear to a job interview? When I am giving a speech on personal branding inevitably somebody will raise this question. You will be judged on what you wear the moment you walk in the door. There are corporate firms who pride themselves on image with strict guidelines and rules dictating dress standards but some other companies are very creative and causal. My advice is to dress for the job and the company so the focus is on you as a person and not your short skirt, unpolished shoes or tired tie. Dressing for a job interview at an advertising agency will differ to one at a corporate law firm. Do some research and ask people who work for the company what the appropriate attire is. If in doubt always dress up — and by this I mean don't dress casually. The most important part of personal branding is to keep clean — clean nails, hair, teeth and clothing. The entire package is the overall look. My tip is also to prepare for things if they go wrong. For example, men should have an extra white shirt ready just in case they cut themselves shaving.

We put time and energy into what we wear when we attend a wedding or a funeral because of our respect for the people involved and the occasion. You should treat your clothes for your presentation and job interview with the same level of attention.

> **'Attitude is everything.'**
> — Diane von Furstenberg, designer

When planning your outfit for your next presentation, look at yourself in a full-length mirror and ask yourself, 'How do I want others to perceive me before I even utter a word?' Then ask someone whose judgment you trust,

'What words describe me based on how I dress?' If you want to be perceived as professional and authoritative and they tell you that you are relaxed and casual, you may want to re-think your outfit. By avoiding obvious clothing distractions and wearing clothing that suits you and your message, you'll ensure your audience remembers what you said, not what you wore.

> *'I have always believed in being very careful about my clothing, because I can then forget about it.'*
> — Frank Lloyd Wright, architect

Choose your clothes carefully. Why? Because you will feel calm and in control. Pay attention to every detail, then you can forget about your image and concentrate on what you are saying. Appropriate clothing also helps the audience to listen to your message instead of focusing on your appearance.

Similarly, worn-out clothes convey the message that you don't care enough. If your audience perceives you as unprofessional, they won't respect you either. The world treats you as you treat yourself.

Dress well and you will send out a signal that you are confident and comfortable in your skin. It does not matter what size you are because there are always clothes to make you look fabulous.

WHAT TO AVOID WHEN PRESENTING ON TELEVISION:

- Stripes or spots.
- See-through clothing.
- Shiny fabric.
- White clothing.
- Busy patterns (unless you are a fashion designer and can get away with it).
- Messy hair and untidy makeup (find out if these will be attended to on the day).

> *'It is the costume that transforms actors into characters.'*
> — Ngila Dixon, Academy and BAFTA award-winning costume designer

WHAT TO AVOID WHEN PRESENTING ON STAGE:

- Very short skirts.
- Noisy bracelets.
- Chipped nail polish.
- Ladders in stockings.
- Dresses if wearing a lapel microphone.
- Messy hair and untidy makeup.
- Tight clothing.
- Ill-fitting suit jackets.
- Untucked shirts.
- Laces undone.
- Gap of skin between shoes and trousers.

How you present your image will and should change, and often that will occur in conjunction with the evolution of your personal brand. I recommend continually decluttering your wardrobe, say every six months, because it sometimes helps to facilitate a re-think of your personal brand and put you back in control of your professional look.

Consider your wardrobe when answering the following questions:

- Are you happy with your current 'look'?
- Did you feel confident with what you wore at the last networking function you attended?
- Do you have a positive body image?
- Do you feel you take pride in your appearance (hair, face, clothing, shoes)?
- Does your clothing reflect your personality as well as your company's brand or culture?

If you are speaking on behalf of your organization, what you wear communicates a message about the company as well as about you. You owe it to your employer to spend some time thinking about the image you project. You are an ambassador for this brand.

Take responsibility and double-check the details of your presentation.

The golden rule is to mirror the audience's dress. If they are formal, dress formally; if casual, dress down.

Style

We are not born with style. We learn how to dress. My personal style has developed by observing others who have expertise in this area, usually friends with exceptional flair.

If there was an award called 'best speech, worst dressed' I have a candidate in mind. I attended a conference and was mesmerized by an entrepreneur's story about how she successfully built her empire. Also at the event was a fashion designer friend and we were both aghast when we saw the speaker's clothing. It was as if she had got dressed in the dark and had grabbed different pieces that didn't go together. Her gaudy and dishevelled appearance was in no way aligned with her brilliant message and personal story. My friend was brave enough to hand her a business card at the end of her speech and I also suggested that she seek help. We understood that this worthy corporate player and keynote speaker was limiting her outreach and impact by wearing distracting clothing. Her wardrobe overshadowed her words.

> *'Fashion fades, style is eternal.'*
> — Yves Saint Laurent, fashion designer

What the experts say

Sue Donnelly is an image consultant in the United Kingdom. I met Sue while I lived in London when interviewing her to work with some of my clients.

Here are her top tips:

- Dress appropriately. Consider the organization, industry, dress code and culture, the event you're attending and your role and objectives.
- Choose quality. Buy the best you can afford. Cheap-looking clothes and accessories will never communicate gravitas.
- Look current. If you look up-to-date on the outside, you will be seen as up-to-date on the inside.

- Show impeccable grooming. Gaining respect from others starts with showing respect for you. Make sure that anything that isn't covered by clothing is clean and smart. Make sure you can move freely, sit down, and walk about without creasing the fabric, tightness, pulling, or too much flesh on show.

- Choose appropriate colours. Colours should flatter your complexion and communicate your intentions. For power and authority, go for a high colour contrast, for example, dark suit, white shirt, red tie; for approachability, go for colours that blend pleasingly to the eye, for example, grey suit, pale blue shirt/blouse.

- Authenticity is key. Clothes should express your personality and what you want to tell the world about yourself. Dress in styles that suit your body shape and complexion. Wear clothes that feel good, look good and give you confidence. Developing a signature style will help you to build a personal brand that says what *you* want to say about yourself. In choosing to adopt a certain style, make sure that the messages you express through your clothes are consistent with how you want to be seen.

Eddie Von Dadelszen is creative director for Working Style, a fashion outlet in New Zealand. He is an expert in men's fashion and I have sought his impeccable styling for male clients. His suggestion is, 'Dressing well most importantly must respond to a sense of self otherwise it doesn't feel genuine. Looking comfortable in your clothes/chosen style always presents better than someone who looks uncomfortable but fashionable. So, a good stylist enhances people's character through clothing and doesn't try and redefine them according to a seasonal trend or idea of whom they think they should look like. You should look like the best possible version of yourself.'

Maintenance

After investing in getting your look just right, how do you make sure you stay looking good right up to the presentation?

Ensure clothes and shoes are ready to be worn before you put them away. Attend to loose buttons and hems or use a trusted dressmaker or drycleaner. Find a good clothes brush — I find the slightly sticky roller type to be the most effective.

Shoes should be regularly re-heeled and polished. Keep good shoes in a shoe bag and use a shoetree to help them keep their shape.

Put together a clothes maintenance kit, including a clothes brush, a small sewing kit, shoe polish/shoe cleaner, needle and cotton. Have it with you at work or when you travel.

TIPS ON WEARING CLOTHES
THAT MAKE YOU FEEL GOOD

- If you are unsure about your style, stick to the classics.
- Make sure your clothes fit properly. Be honest about your body, and ask for feedback from people you trust. If store-bought clothes don't fit you properly, have them tailored. If you can afford it, get something made for you by a fashion designer that specializes in bespoke tailoring.
- Regularly declutter your wardrobe. Give away or throw out clothing that doesn't fit well.
- Avoid excessive fragrance or cologne, as it can be overpowering.
- Clothing must be spotless and pressed. Worn-out and tired clothing makes you look lazy and unprofessional.
- Wear comfortable, high-quality shoes, and maintain them well. Scruffy, worn-out or dirty shoes distract the audience from your message.
- Remember to dress lightly when giving a speech, as stress can raise your body temperature. However, always take a jacket just in case the temperature changes.
- Invest in quality garments. Your clothing will last longer, so it's cheaper in the long run.
- Keep on wearing your favourite colours that make you feel good.

FOR WOMEN

- Avoid heavy makeup — go for the natural look. However, my advice is to wear at least a little makeup if you're comfortable doing so, to avoid looking washed out.

- Make sure the audience can see your eyes. If you have a fringe don't hide behind it. Allow yourself to see and be seen.
- Provocative clothing is a real no-no — it undermines your credibility.
- Avoid very high shoes — the simpler the better. You want the focus to be on you not your accessories.
- Keep your nails well manicured. Have a regular manicure or set aside time each week to maintain your nails yourself. When you gesture, the audience will notice your hands, so your nails need to be immaculate.
- If you wear open-toe shoes in the summer make sure your toenails are tidy. Regular visits to a podiatrist or a nail bar are a good investment.
- Keep a spare pair of pantyhose in your bag in case you get a last-minute ladder.
- The higher the stage is, the shorter your skirt will appear. Ideal skirt hems are at mid-knee or slightly below, depending on your work culture.
- 'The sense of being well-dressed gives a feeling of inner tranquility.' — C.F. Forbes, writer

FOR MEN

- Make sure that your socks go under your trousers so that no skin is showing.
- Make sure your shirt isn't hanging out.
- Wear good-quality ties and replace them when they're looking worn out.
- Make sure the tie pattern isn't distracting to the audience. Cufflinks are a more subtle way of expressing your personality.
- If wearing a suit, consider expressing your personality by wearing colourful socks.

16
Specialist Speeches

'My people, my people, listen!'

— Martin Luther King Jr, civil rights activist

For some of you, speaking at a wedding, funeral or office farewell will be the most nerve-racking public-speaking experience of all because of the emotions attached to the occasion. It is normal to be more anxious about speaking in front of people you know and care about rather than an audience you may never see again. Over the years, I have had many clients ask for help preparing to speak at family functions, especially weddings and funerals. The public-speaking basics discussed throughout the book apply equally to these situations. This chapter will give you a few extra tips to make this important speech a winner. Have a look at Chapter 6 on developing and writing content, which will also help you to structure your speech and has useful tips to get you started.

Accept invitations to speak

'When power corrupts, poetry cleanses.'

— John F. Kennedy, former US president

I encourage you to accept invitations to speak at family and social events — it's an honour to be asked to contribute and it obviously means a lot to the person asking you or they wouldn't have chosen you. These types of speeches are also a great opportunity to practise your public-speaking skills in front of a sympathetic and supportive audience. Acknowledge that you might feel vulnerable, especially at a funeral where you are emotionally involved, and have the courage to speak regardless — you'll be so pleased you did. I read a poem at my grandmother's funeral after she died at age 99. It was a special time for me as I had a deep respect for this matriarch. I wrote some words leading me into the poem and finished with a few personal words. The choice of a poignant poem or piece of prose can speak for you and help to reduce the stress of standing up in front of family and loved ones. I have employed this practice of weaving poems and quotes into the eulogies and remembrance speeches I have delivered and it has always helped to relax me.

More and more political leaders are starting to hire presentation and media coaches. My friend and former colleague, Labour MP Stuart Nash, is known as a confident speaker but it wasn't always that way. This is his story.

'A very important part of being a politician is being able to clearly communicate ideas and messages that resonate with voters. Being a competent public speaker in a way that engages an audience is a key competency for an MP. Throughout school and university I was involved in debating and public speaking, so when I first entered parliament I thought I could deliver a pretty good speech. In my first speech I didn't know the rules and was heckled mercilessly by experienced government MPs. I sat down after 5 minutes, shattered and drained of all confidence.

'For the next four months, whenever I was on the party's speaking list for a Bill in Parliament, I spent 2 to 3 hours preparing for a 10-minute speech, and at least an hour preparing for a 5-minute speech. When my turn to stand up came, I read word-for-word. This was totally unsustainable, so I sought the counsel of a very senior Labour MP. He gave me some hints, and whenever possible, critiqued my speeches for the next few months. By the end of my first three-year term, I had given more speeches in the House than any Labour MP! I could pick up a piece of legislation I had no idea about, spend 10 minutes writing a couple of relevant messages and stand up and deliver time and time again. Where others shied away, I sought speaking opportunities.

'In the 30 months it took to get there, I gave some pretty terrible speeches, but with each one my ability to articulate key points in a concise manner developed; most importantly, my confidence in my ability to give a speech on nearly anything, anywhere, anytime grew. I only got there by practising — week in and week out. Literally throwing myself outside my comfort zone and taking on the challenge of becoming a good speaker inside and outside parliament. There really is only one way to become great, and that is to practise. Take any opportunity to stand up and deliver a presentation, give a speech, lead the discussion and put forward your ideas.'

Stuart's great-grandfather, Sir Walter Nash, was prime minister of New Zealand from 1950 to 1968. Sir Walter would be proud of his great-grandson!

Funerals

'There is a sacredness in tears. They are not the mark of weakness, but of power. They speak more eloquently than ten thousand tongues. They are the messengers of overwhelming grief, of deep contrition, and of unspeakable love.' — Washington Irving, writer

It is a great honour to be asked to speak at a funeral, whether you are giving the main eulogy or a supporting speech, or simply saying a few words about the deceased. Find out what is expected of you. How long will you be speaking for? Have you been asked to talk about the life and achievements of your loved one or friend, or your personal memories of him or her? Ask how many people will be speaking — you won't want to talk for too long if there are five more people speaking after you.

The key to a successful eulogy, as with any speech, is research and preparation. This is one occasion where you don't want to wing it as it's disrespectful and you won't do your best. Write down your speech and have it with you in case you lose your place. Lastly, if the speech is longer than 5 minutes, make sure you rehearse it out loud as you may find that some pieces are difficult to say or don't flow as they should, and the rehearsal will give you the opportunity to rephrase them before the funeral.

If your speech is about the life and achievements of the person, ask the family if there is anything they'd prefer you didn't mention. A funeral is not the time to settle old scores or score points. Also, be sensitive about using humour, as there will be a wide range of people in the audience and an anecdote that raises a smile among a person's friends may be offensive to their grandparents. Don't feel bad about crying during the delivery of the eulogy — if it happens, it happens. Just be you. Worrying about it is likely to distract you from saying what you want to say. I find it helps to remember that the eulogy isn't about the person delivering the speech; it is about remembering a life and sharing it with family and friends. You are not speaking to gain approval or to please in any way. If you focus on your audience and its needs, your speech is likely to soothe, move hearts and provide comfort.

When you are looking for material to include in a eulogy, go with your gut instinct. There are many poetry collections and reference books to quote from, and a search on the internet will also provide ideas, although they won't all be to your liking. Perhaps there is an author whom the deceased person used to particularly enjoy or a piece of writing that is relevant to their life? For example, New Zealand sailor and adventurer Sir Peter Blake was shot and killed by pirates while monitoring environmental change in the Amazon. He was arguably the world's greatest around-the-world sailor and at his memorial service, his children read 'Bilbo's Last Song' from *The Lord of the Rings* by J.R.R. Tolkien, a poem about a sailor saying farewell to his home and friends, and following a star above his mast. It was the perfect choice.

Whenever I've read the following poem at a funeral, people have asked me for copies. I've included it here in case it's of use to you one day or to share with friends and family. It's positive and the meaning is universal.

WHEN WE REMEMBER
By David Harkins

You can shed tears that she is gone or you can smile because she has lived.

You can close your eyes and pray that she'll come back or you can open your eyes and see all she's left.

Your heart can be empty because you can't see her or you can be full of the love you shared.

You can turn your back on tomorrow and live yesterday or you can be happy for tomorrow because of yesterday.

You can remember her and only that she is gone or you can cherish her memory and let it live on.

You can cry and close your mind, be empty and turn your back or you can do what she'd want:

Smile,

Open your eyes,

Love and go on.

Weddings

Wedding speeches seem to bring out the best and worst in public speakers. It's such a joyous occasion and the best wedding speeches hit the right notes of celebration, humour and love that deeply touch the couple and the rest of the audience. But the worst speeches, where the great-uncle drones on for half an hour, or the best man or best woman regales the audience with sexist jokes, make you cringe with embarrassment. There are a few simple rules to follow if you are asked to give a speech at a wedding to ensure yours is one of the successful ones.

Weddings traditionally had three main speakers: the bride's father, the groom and the best man. However, weddings today are often anything but traditional and it has become usual for a variety of people to speak.

It is very important to ask what material you are expected to cover and how long you are to speak for. It's unlikely that you'll be expected to give a thorough retelling of their life stories from birth to the present day. You may be asked to make a toast to a particular person, to provide some information about the couple, or to simply wish them well. Whatever the expectation, it's crucial that you know it.

The usual public-speaking rules of research, preparation and rehearsal are fundamental to wedding speeches. This is a very important day, so treat the occasion with respect and do your homework.

Michael Dunlop, my former boss in my PR days, is a confident speaker and is frequently asked to make a speech at family weddings. His main tip is to do thorough research before the day. 'I ask questions such as what is the style of the wedding, what are your expectations of my speech, what kind of things are important to you? It's important to understand the impact your words will have on the guests attending. Create the appropriate impact for the nature of the occasion and consider the people there. Every wedding is unique as this is the only time that this particular group of people will ever come together. They are nervous, so your role is to also break down barriers.'

Inappropriate speeches

Some people seem to think it's appropriate to bring up the worst and most embarrassing moments in their wedding speech. I recall feeling so disappointed after witnessing the 'roasting' of the groom at a wedding as most of the stories seemed to involve drunken escapades that might have been amusing to people in the stories, but certainly weren't funny to the rest of the audience.

Equally embarrassing are stories with obvious sexual undertones — there is no need to get cheap laughs. It adds nothing to such a special event. During one such speech, the unconscious body language of the mother of the bride and the mother of the groom showed their horrified reaction to the best man's speech, which was trying to entertain by being funny at the expense of the bride and the groom. Don't bring up past partners, racist or sexist comments or stag-night antics and watch out for your own bias, such as a phobia about marriage.

A wedding is a time when people gather to celebrate and rejoice, not to mock. It is a privilege to speak at someone's wedding, as it's not something that happens very often in your life. You were chosen because you're considered to be a special part of the couple's life. They are relying on your heartfelt speech to create more magic on their day.

Know your audience and rehearse your speech in front of a family member if you are unsure about including sensitive material. And follow the golden rule — if in doubt, leave it out.

Time and effort pay off

Spend time thinking about the special qualities of the couple, noting stories that are real, funny, moving and inspiring. Show the human side of each person so that the audience gets to see their unique qualities.

I recall coaching a client who was nervous about speaking at his daughter's wedding. He wanted to get it right so decided to ask for professional advice. We spent 2 hours mapping out the key messages he wanted to communicate. I suggested he think about a wonderful story describing her as a child and find a superb baby photo or a photo of her doing something exceptional and weave this visual element into the material. He decided to use PowerPoint at the reception so he could have some photos behind him as he spoke. His confidence grew as we worked on ideas and structure. After the speech, members of the audience congratulated him, saying it was one of the best speeches they had ever heard. Speaking in public was a major challenge for him, and the successful outcome was due to the effort he put into his preparation.

Putting nervousness into perspective

Peter Beck, former Dean of Christchurch Cathedral, is also an experienced wedding celebrant. A confident speaker, Peter recalls a story about a groom overcome by nervousness during his wedding vows:

'One groom was so struck by the immensity of what he was doing that in the middle of his vows — and he was going well — he started to sweat, paled and suddenly fainted straight into my arms! So, out came a chair and a glass of water, of course, and there in front of everyone we fanned and chatted, and smiled and spoke about this never-to-be-forgotten moment, until he was able to stand up again. With great purpose and determination he did what he had to and wanted to do so much: made his vow and loved his bride. A great cheer went up and some said afterwards that it was the best wedding they had ever been to!'

If this groom can overcome this degree of nervousness, surely you can overcome yours!

Ideas for wedding speeches

- Aim for a warm tone.

- Find a link between a key event in the year the couple were born and weave it into the opening of your speech.

- Interview family members and friends about their wishes for the couple, and advice for the future — you might find a few gems you can borrow.

- What happened on the day in history? There may be a momentous event that happened 50 years ago. Just make sure the event is a happy one!

- Don't include 'in-jokes' as everyone present should be able to understand what you're talking about.

- Keep the jokes and anecdotes clean, relevant and short, and don't laugh at your own jokes.

- Ending on a toast gives you something to work towards and provides a clear ending to your speech.

Tips for a successful wedding speech

- Give a copy of the speech to another guest before the big day and ask them to bring it with them just in case you lose yours. Don't rely on your memory.

- Practise the speech on film to hear if it sounds stilted and needs rephrasing.

- Stay off the alcohol until after your speech. You might not think you're drunk but even a tipsy speaker is embarrassing to watch.

- Have an early night the night before so you are fresh for the big day.

- Keep it brief. Ten minutes is probably long enough.

Other family celebrations

Other occasions where you might be asked to give a speech include milestone birthdays, anniversaries and christenings. The same rules apply — prepare well and think carefully about what you want to say. Speeches made on these occasions are remembered for many years, so make sure they are remembered for all the right reasons!

My brother Tony recalls speaking at his daughters' twenty-first birthday celebrations. 'I wanted firstly to honour them as individuals but also in a family and community context. To me their twenty-firsts were celebrations of transitions in life — their journeys from childhood and adolescence to womanhood. I was conscious of the many friends and other significant people in my daughters' lives who were present to share in their celebration. So I also wanted to use these occasions to stir in them some of those deep yearnings of the heart that help make sense of life. To achieve this, I drew on memories of childhood, imagery in nature and the concept of dreams. For both my daughters I also incorporated significant music and poetry into my talks to intensify my feelings about this important milestone in their lives.'

I can confirm that the speeches were beautiful and heartfelt, and much appreciated by each daughter.

Thank you speeches

Thank you speeches are sometimes planned and sometimes impromptu, depending on the circumstances. If you know it's coming up, prepare and rehearse as for any other speech. If it's a surprise, try to remember the following points.

- Thank everyone as a group and a few key people individually, rather than listing a large number of people.
- Say why you are thanking the person or audience.
- Keep it simple and succinct — a gracious thank you and exit is far more compelling than a half-hour ramble.

However, if you have been honoured for something that has taken a lot of work or a lifetime achievement, you may like to outline some of the work you've done, or prepare a speech themed around the goals of the organization you've worked for.

Toasts

The dictionary defines a toast as 'a tribute or proposal of health and success, marked by raising glasses and drinking together'. Giving a toast might seem easy, but if you haven't thought it through, it's easy to go blank at the crucial moment. Talk to the person who has asked you to make the toast to see if they have any specific requirements. What do they want your toast to achieve? A toast should only be 2 to 3 minutes long, so be sure to time yourself during rehearsal and cut your speech back if necessary.

Deliver the toast standing up, and be aware that you may have your back to some people. If so, consider moving to the front of the room or at least acknowledging the people behind you before starting to speak. When you have finished, raise your glass, say, 'To Granny' (or whoever) and take a drink. This action signals the end of the speech.

Welcome speeches at work

If you are introducing a new colleague to the company, make sure you know a little about him or her — how to pronounce their name, what they'll be doing at the company and a little about their background.

Your goal during the speech is to put your new colleague at ease. Remember how you felt during your first week at work. Be sincere and make an effort to put thought into your welcome speech.

Farewell speeches at work

When farewelling a work colleague, your goal is to send that person on their way on a high note and feeling acknowledged. While amusing stories may be funny, make sure they do not mock or humiliate the person. Mention what you've learned from working with the person and underline the impact he or she has made on co-workers and the overall contribution to the organization.

Commemorative speeches

'Tell me, what else should I have done?
Doesn't everything die at last, and too soon?
Tell me, what is it you plan to do
With your one wild and precious life?'
— Mary Oliver, American poet

Commemorative speeches require intimate and yet also poetic and stirring language. They can also be tricky because of the emotional nature of the event and circumstances of someone's death.

My brother asked me to attend a commemorative occasion remembering three World War II pilots including our cousin, William Hodgson. They died in an accident in 1941 after the Battle of Britain. I was to deliver a speech on my family's behalf after nearly two days of travelling from New Zealand to London and then on the train to Essex. I was completely exhausted and had no idea that this event was such a big deal and that there would be media present. I was also surprised at the emotional upsurge that I experienced giving the speech in the church and going to the gravesite. I sobbed when I saw my cousin's grave at the Saffron Walden cemetery, thinking about his mother in the 1940s who never had the opportunity to bury her own son.

The lesson here is that during solemn or commemorative speeches, be prepared for unexpected emotions to arise. Take your time, pause, breathe and speak when ready.

Inspirational speeches

'There is no greater agony than bearing an
untold story inside you.'
— Maya Angelou, poet, author and actor

We have all been inspired by illustrious language and moving ideas that are poetically and artfully expressed. We remember stirring speeches that move us to our core whether we were there to hear them delivered, saw them on TV or online, or read them in the pages of history. From Socrates to Julius Caesar; John F. Kennedy to Martin Luther King Jr; and Maya Angelou to Benazir Bhutto, who was the first woman to lead a Muslim country, extraordinary oratory is everywhere. If you are asked to give an inspirational speech, set aside some time to immerse yourself in the words of others who delivered speeches that have become legendary. I do this a lot. Two of my recent favourites come from women whom I admire for their leadership, courage and authentic female voices. I encourage you to look them up online and take a listen.

- Former Australian Prime Minister Julia Gillard's speech to parliament when she was serving as the country's first female prime minister. It went viral and made headlines around the globe even as she was being bullied and put down at home, especially by then opposition leader Tony Abbott. 'I will not be lectured about sexism and misogyny by this man,' Gillard said, motioning towards Mr Abbott. 'If he wants to know what misogyny looks like in modern Australia, he doesn't need a motion in the House of Representatives, he needs a mirror.'

- United States First Lady Michelle Obama's speech in April 2015 at an event hosted by Black Entertainment Television proclaiming Black Girls Rock! 'Yes, I decided to rewrite those tired old scripts that define too many of us. I decided that I wasn't bossy, I was confident and strong. I wasn't loud, I was a young woman with something important to say and when I looked in the mirror I saw a tall, beautiful and smart black girl ... and that's what I want for you, I want you to live life on your own terms ... but anyone who's achieved anything in life knows that challenges and failures are necessary components of success. They know that when things get hard, that's not always a sign that you're doing something wrong, that's often a sign that you're doing something right. Those hard times are what shape you into the person you're meant to be.'

Another of my favourite speakers is my friend Alain Roth. Born in Paris, Alain travelled the world leading seminars for a global training company. He spoke in his second language, English, to groups of over 200 people and could move me and his audience to laughter, tears, reflection, sadness and joy with a simple raise of his eyebrow. Watching him lead a seminar that ran for three consecutive 12-hour days was like being absorbed in a movie you never wanted to end.

How did he do it? Without a doubt his success lay in his delivery. He shared his stories with vigour and liveliness. His body language was never static. His voice travelled with passion; his eyes transmitted words; his contagious smile put us at ease. He grinned endearingly and spoke with raw guts. He made us laugh again and again using the pure wit and spontaneity that flows naturally from stories.

Observing experienced speakers like Alain can help us all become better speakers. They are not concerned with ego and looking good. They take risks. Such speakers will always move us to tears because we feel that they really care about us and not about themselves.

Master of Ceremonies

As a Master of Ceremonies, your job is to be the link between the different speakers or events. You are the glue that holds the function together, so you'll need to be well briefed about the format, and confident enough to think on your feet if things go off track. The success of your MC experience will depend on how much you know about the function and what is expected of you, so you can properly prepare.

As you are introducing other speakers, you need to know a little about them. Take the time to talk to each speaker before the occasion, if possible, and ask how he or she would like to be introduced. Think of yourself as the link between speeches when scripting your own material.

Keep it short. The MC is not the main event. If you talk for too long, the audience will become restless before the main speakers have even started. Keep the mood fun and upbeat.

Ask for an agenda and stick to it. Your job is to keep the event on track. To do this you should be able to command the attention of an audience. You might like to have a watch on the lectern so you can nod to speakers when you need them to wrap up their presentation. This may not always be appropriate though, so ask in advance what the organizer would like you to do if speakers take longer than their allotted time.

TIPS ON SPEAKING AT FAMILY EVENTS

- **Prepare for a speech at a family event** just as thoroughly as you would for a business function.

- **Your speech should focus on the reason** for the event, not on you.

- **Approach the speech with respect, empathy and love** and you won't go wrong.

- **If in doubt, ask.** Make sure you know what's expected of you.

- **No sexist, racist or inappropriate jokes**, especially if you are presenting to a diverse group of people.

- **Use stories and examples** to make your points. They will help transform your speech into a glowing performance.

- **Be memorable** — it's your choice how you and your speech will be remembered.

17
Speaking Confidently to the Media

'The public have an insatiable curiosity to know everything, except what is worth knowing. Journalism, conscious of this, and having tradesman-like habits, supplies their demands.'

— Oscar Wilde, writer and social commentator

At best the contemporary media scene is complex and constantly changing; at worst it is chaotic and challenging. My advice is: do your homework, get some training, zip your lips until you've engaged your brain.

The word 'media' no longer describes the seemingly old-fashioned concept of 'mainstream media' where print, radio and television selected and produced a daily diet of news, information and entertainment for local, national and international audiences. Now, journalists operate across all media platforms while the rest of the world feeds them, outsmarts them and overwhelms them from almost every imaginable point of view, from vitriolic and abusive to supportive and sycophantic.

Today's media embraces much of what can be said and seen online or on mobile devices, and journalists constantly monitor the online space for breaking news, embarrassing leaks, wacko tweets, and anything else weird or wonderful they can turn into a story. Obviously there's far more interaction between the public and various sections of the media than ever before, as millions of daily tweets and Facebook posts comment on stories, and commentators and bloggers respond to each other and to the public. (See the technology section in Chapter 12.)

What this means is that whether the media come to you (reactive media) or you go to them (proactive media) it pays to understand how they operate, what they want and what makes a story.

This is not as easy as it sounds. As more and more journalists lose their jobs, there are fewer and fewer of them in newsrooms and they are less able to chase stories and deal with inquiries. Increasingly, they are gathering news online but the magnitude of what's out there is overwhelming and they rely more and more on news from 'tried and true' experts and from the natural selection that creates the daily news agenda.

At one level, it's never been easier for people to get news of one kind or another into the media; at another level, it's a very complex arena, so people and organizations who want to engage and make a good job of it need to commit time and money to the task.

Although there are fewer opportunities for you to get your news and views into the mainstream media, there are many channels you can use in the digital or online space: TEDx, online video posts, Facebook posts, tweets and more dynamic interactive websites are all examples of what communication-savvy organizations are doing. However, doing these things well is the trick and that all comes down to great presentation.

Things that can damage your reputation

Everyone knows the story about the public relations executive, Justine Sacco, who sparked outrage when she tweeted, 'Going to Africa. Hope I don't get AIDS. Just Kidding. I'm White!' Personally I think this is the most offensive tweet I have ever read. The tweet was re-tweeted over 3000 times and picked up by media outlets all around the world before she even got off the plane. It is no surprise that she was fired from her job despite making a public apology. We live in a world where anything you say now online will inevitably end up in the media if it's newsworthy. This woman's reputation has been damaged forever. In an event like this, if you are not a journalist or public relations consultant you need to access someone who specializes in media crisis and damage control. 'I'm sorry' goes a long way — if you can say it in time. This is why it's so important to get some media training before you agree to any media interview because you will learn about all the things that could go wrong that you would never otherwise think about.

These are the kinds of issues that frequently show up in our media training sessions. They're common all over the world. Notice how they're nearly all about reputation.

- Companies in the spotlight for bad customer service, poor treatment of staff, tax dodges or financial malpractice.
- Personalities the public 'loves to love or hate' exposed for sexual harassment, dodgy financial dealings, dubious online behaviour, duplicity or lack of integrity.
- Sports stars, politicians, media and entertainment stars who get drunk, take drugs, cheat on their partners, or lose the plot online.
- Institutions that waste public money, are not accountable for their actions and use 'weasel words' to get themselves out of tight corners.

I have to say we have just as many clients who believe in what they're doing, want to tell their story, have something to say, and need help to do it effectively. The problem here is that they often don't understand that an issue is *not* a story. A story needs to:

- Paint a picture and be told in lively, engaging language.
- Engage an audience, and use the right channels to do so.
- Be told persuasively.

A good story requires time, though, planning and practice. These things are never easy to deliver at speed when you're under pressure from an increasingly complex and competitive media.

Building relationships with the media

Overall, your starting point is to be friendly and professional. Find out who's who in your patch, what they're looking for, when their deadlines are, and what is the best way to engage with them. Work at building a rapport with key journalists and try to interest them in what you do, why you do it, and how that can translate into stories that fit their formats.

- Take time to meet journalists, call them, or send a friendly email.
- Respond professionally and quickly to inquiries.
- If you can't help, suggest someone who can.
- Avoid a 'no comment' response — if you can't comment give a reason.
- Treat the media with respect. You also have the same right to respect, professionalism and honesty.
- If you can't afford media training, learn from others who've dealt with the media, or look for the by-lines of journalists whose work you admire and contact them.
- If you're sending story ideas, cut to the chase and sell them in a lively and interesting way and back your assertions with facts.

'Put it before them briefly so they will read it, clearly so they will appreciate it, picturesquely so they will remember it and, above all, accurately so they will be guided by its light.' — Joseph Pulitzer, publisher

What makes news?

Frequently journalists tell me that important, potentially groundbreaking speeches fail to hit the mark because writers and speechmakers don't understand what makes news.

The media is always looking for something that tells a curious public something new. If it's 'new', it's just happened, it's about to happen or was only recently discovered. News must interest, entertain and engage its audience. Think about these three things:

- MAGNITUDE. How big is the story? How many people has it affected?
- PROMINENCE. Does it involve someone in the world whom your country or community knows, and sees as a public figure or personality?
- CONSEQUENCE. What are the ongoing consequences of this event, discovery, scandal or announcement?

People are interested in other people. Stories about people help us connect on a human level. Variations on the human interest story always work a treat: winners and losers, the extraordinary achievements of the ordinary, and the ordinary lives of the extraordinary, all make good stories.

Other things that make news are heart, reputation, money (making it, raking it, losing it or abusing it), research, reports and statistics, opinion, politics, conflict and change.

In many parts of the world, the top Google searches of 2014 included: the FIFA World Cup, Robin Williams' suicide, Malaysia Airlines (MH370), iPhone 6, and Ebola. See how these all fit in with the various categories I've listed.

Have something to say

When a journalist calls they usually want *information*, *confirmation* (that something has or hasn't happened) or *opinion*. They regard you as an 'expert' and want you to say something that they can attribute as your opinion, your 'take' on the issue, or your account of what's just happened.

What the media sees as news might not seem like news to you but it is to the public. Maybe it's something you've done for years, a practice your company has regularly undertaken, or 'business as usual' wherever you work. Remember that very few people have run a soup kitchen, worked a Saturday night shift in a hospital emergency department, been an actor or driven a fire truck.

Remember:

- You will nearly always know more about the issue than the media.

- A journalist's job is to get a variety of opinions, so don't expect to get a perfect précis of your point of view. They'll nearly always be looking for others.

- Be careful about 'talking off the record'. The journalist is talking to you to get a story, so unless you have demonstrable evidence that they are trustworthy expect everything to be 'on the record'.

Preparation pays off

Preparation is the key to success for just about everything in life. On our courses we routinely see evidence of how preparation makes a difference. A simple rule is to never walk blindly into media interviews without thinking about what you're doing!

Why do you think politicians appear so confident on television? They are used to it, and have the opportunity to practise regularly. This is why I encourage anyone in business to take regular media-training refreshers so that when the real interview turns up you are ready to go. Think of yourself as an athlete: you need to keep your skills sharpened.

Get some perspective

'A good leader can engage in a debate frankly and thoroughly, knowing that at the end he and the other side must be closer, and thus emerge stronger. You don't have that idea when you are arrogant, superficial, and uninformed.' — Nelson Mandela, former South African president and human rights activist

No matter what issue you're discussing, being interviewed can seem overwhelming at times. Even professionals can make mistakes. Learn from them. Try to see media interviews as opportunities to develop news skills and pass on experiences and stories to potential new clients. Nerves are natural but you can manage them.

The same goes for reading about yourself in a print or online media. In an *Australian Women's Weekly* interview, former New Zealand prime minister Helen Clark put it this way: 'You have to have a bit of a deaf ear to get on. Keep looking straight ahead and don't be distracted. You are a prime minster dealing with big issues and someone wants to talk about whether your teeth are straight — get over it.'

When the media calls

Journalists do the majority of their work on the phone. Most often they'll want to interview you as soon as they call. Alternatively they may want to organize a face-to-face interview at a later time.

When you receive a media call see it as the beginning of a contract. Your role is not to do the interview then and there; it is to find out more about what they want and decide on a course of action.

If you have communications staff or a PR agency available to you, they will generally receive in-coming media calls and set up interviews for you. If you receive the media call first, consider the following and find out:

- Who's calling and where they work. Journalists must always identify themselves and say who they work for.

- What they want — an interview, background information, your opinion, a comment on someone else's viewpoint, news release, Facebook post or tweet?

- Their deadline. Is it in the next news bulletin, an hour's time, next month?

- How long the interview will be — preparing for a 2-minute interview is very different to preparing for a 20-minute interview on a specialist subject.

- Who else they are talking to? Are you being framed as the 'good guys' or the 'bad guys'? Are you answering allegations of bad behaviour, misconduct, injury or death?

- What's driving their inquiry. Is it another media story, a news release from someone else, a Facebook post, tweet or a piece of recently released research?

Your objective is to be friendly and professional but keep asking questions and be assertive until you are clear about what is wanted. Now *buy time* and thank them for their call.

- Say you're busy, in a meeting, tied up, or need to get more information.
- Tell them you'll ring back (when you do this depends on when their deadline is).
- Ask them to email you a short set of question areas they want to talk to you about.
- Be reliable about honouring agreements you make.
- Call your communication advisor and plan an approach for the interview.

You have just bought enough time to focus on what you want/need to say. Here are some questions to work through on your own or with your communications team.

- Should you do the interview?
- Is it in your interests/the interests of the organization? Do you/they need it?
- How will it come across if you don't do it? Will it be bad for your reputation or the image of your company or organization?
- Are you responsible/does the buck stop with you? If you are responsible, you should always try to front-up early. Avoiding the media is a bad look and nearly always keeps the media engaged and the story alive for much longer.
- Do you have the time? There's nothing worse than a reluctant interviewee, constantly monitoring his mobile phone and looking irritated about the time it's taking. Doing good media

interviews takes time — don't do them if you haven't got it. See if you can do it on another day, or find someone else.

- Do you have the authority/a mandate to speak for your group?

If you/your team decide you should do the interview, here are some pointers to help you prepare:

- Find the key facts to support your argument/issue. The media is always interested in quantitative information — how much, how many, how often, when did this last happen, how was it this time last year?
- Decide what you want to say and develop a priority list with the most important point first. You're better to workshop three or four good points and talk about them well, than create a lengthy list that simply confuses you.
- Isolate your most important message — 'the one thing' you want to get across if you can say nothing else. It's sometimes called the SOCO or 'single overriding communications objective'.
- Think about the worst question you could be asked. Prepare an answer and rehearse it.
- Think about examples you can provide to support your case or illustrate your story.
- If possible, rehearse the whole interview with someone else in the organization or your communications team.
- Be prepared to make your point whether you're asked a question about it or not.

The LART formula is a helpful strategy.

- **LISTEN** to the question.
- **ACKNOWLEDGE** that there is a valid point of view or criticism.
- **REFOCUS** using words like 'however' or the 'key issue is'.
- **TALK**

The CAP formula is a great technique for dealing with various situations involving 'crisis management'; for example, fraud, a major workplace accident or death. Here's how it works.

- **CARE AND CONCERN.** Acknowledge the people, families, workers, or members of the community who are bereft, upset or grief-stricken by what's happened.
- **ACTION.** Outline your plan of action for dealing with the event/crisis. Keep it strong, simple and clear. Under-promise and over-deliver.
- **PERSPECTIVE.** Give a general perspective on what's usual or the norm for your organization.

What to do in a television interview

First up, find out what the media is planning to do.

- Is it a studio interview, a filmed interview, a live or a pre-recorded interview, a news story, or a feature story?
- Who else will be involved?
- What's their timeframe?

Next, plan your approach

- Arrive at the studio/location early.
- Make sure you have back-up phone numbers for the producer and reporter.
- Find out in advance about entry to the building, who will meet you, parking and other practical details.
- Take advantage of makeup even if you don't normally wear it.
- Take time to focus on your interview, rehearse and practise your answers before you get to the studio.
- Ask the journalist/producer if there have been any changes in approach since you last spoke.
- Be friendly and professional.
- Be careful about giving away new information.

- Don't enter into 'off the record' conversations.
- Take someone with you for feedback and support.

Going into the studio

- Get rid of your books and papers — just take one small card with key notes/ statistics on it.
- Turn off your mobile phone.
- Never take a pen you can click
- Sit back in your seat — posture is important.
- Don't sit on a swivel chair.
- Tidy up your jacket, hair and tie.
- Take pens, swipe cards and other distractions out of your pockets.
- Look at the interviewer, not the camera.
- Remember you are likely to be on-camera from the moment you are mic'd until your microphone is taken off.
- Ask the journalist what his/her first question is likely to be. They won't always tell you, but if they will this allows you time to think about your possible answer.

Other helpful hints

Give examples

Volunteer information. An interview always needs good interplay between the interviewer and the interviewee. The interviewer's role is to start the interview, keep it going and end it. It shouldn't be a 'doctor–patient' interview where the interviewer constantly has to 'extract' information from you. Here are some ideas:

- 'One of the most important things about this issue is …'
- 'People may be interested to know …'
- 'One of the most fascinating things about this case is …'
- 'Only yesterday, one of our clients told me …'

- 'A really good example is …'
- 'I can't talk about this case, but some of the most common reasons we see people are …'
- 'Our volunteers frequently tell us …'

Tell stories

Think of a story or an example for the two or three major points you want to make.

Stories help to engage your audience, and you will come across as a human being. Frequently, the story in your interview will be 'the bit' the journalist uses.

Speak visually

- 'It's the size of two rugby fields' is better than: 'The building will cover 2.7 hectares of land.'
- 'When we'd finished the case we had 24 volumes of evidence stacked up against the wall' is better than: 'There was an overwhelming volume of evidence forwarded to the Commission.'

Relate to your audience

- Think from the 'outside in' rather than the 'inside out'. Always ask yourself how you can make your story interesting to someone who knows nothing about it.
- Remember you are communicating with the general public, not your colleagues at work. How would you explain it to your next-door neighbour's sixteen-year-old daughter?
- 'One thing most people don't understand is …'
- 'People who don't live in Nepal and who haven't been through the earthquake may not realize …'

Dump the jargon

Find plain English to replace your jargon and technical terms. (See Chapter 6 on developing and writing content, and for more information on jargon.)

Learn to summarize

In our sessions we teach clients to understand what they can say in different lengths of time. Quite quickly they learn to cut to the chase and make their key points — frequently called 'soundbites' — much more quickly. Soundbites need to be self-contained, accurate, brief and memorable. They are usually 12 to 20 seconds long. These are the bits that if, well done, are edited out of your interview and used in the final news story, they could also be quotes in a print story.

EXERCISE

1. Work in pairs.
2. Pick a topic — this could be business related or personal.
3. Face each other and label yourselves 'A' and 'B'.
4. Get someone to time you.
5. Person A goes first and has 12 to 20 seconds to make their statement about the chosen topic.
6. Person B listens, watches, and notes the bits of the message that work.
7. When the time is up, Person B gives feedback to Person A.
8. Now swap roles.
9. Person A gives feedback to Person B.
10. Repeat the exercise, both ways, in only 15 seconds.
11. If you have time, give a final presentation of your statement to a small audience.

This is a great way to become confident and learn what works.

While it's good practice to never rote learn your answer, you need to be able to talk naturally and be nimble enough to answer questions you're not expecting — or, answer them in a different way. I recall a conversation with a producer of a television news show who joked, 'I don't want you polishing your clients up too much.' I laughed and told him we were simply helping people to feel more relaxed and ready for questions, which in turn helped the interviewers to do their job.

Anticipate the tough questions and prepare for them

What are the five curliest questions you might be asked? Practise your answers. Role-play with a colleague until you are more comfortable with your response. Our experience is that difficult questions invariably produce better interviews than those littered with 'patsy' questions.

The eyes have it

Always maintain eye contact with the journalist. Eyes darting at the floor or ceiling can make you look shifty or nervous; you want the viewers to relate to you and think you're trustworthy.

Don't panic if the interviewer is not looking at you. Keep on looking at him or her. You're more likely to 'read' the interviewer's body language if you focus on them. Never look down the camera lens when giving answers.

I notice this is often one of the most difficult things to change. In real life we don't always maintain eye contact. We talk and reflect on our thoughts and often have our eyes elsewhere. So, practising eye contact can seem false. Don't worry. With practice, you will find that looking people in the eye becomes natural, even powerful. Try focusing on just one eye. It's not a staring-down session, so if the other person becomes uncomfortable, look away momentarily. Study their body language. If this makes you lose attention and miss what they're saying, focus on their mouth and their words. Then when it's your turn to speak, return to their eyes so they can see you speak with integrity.

Warm-up

BE AWARE OF YOUR BODY LANGUAGE

Good posture is important. Sit up straight. Pull your shoulders back. Stand tall and you'll breathe correctly and appear confident. Avoid hunching up. Your diaphragm needs to be able to do its job. Bad posture will lead to shallow breathing, less oxygen flowing to the brain, and your responses will slow.

Look confident and be yourself. Spontaneous gestures make you look expressive but there is nothing worse than gesturing for the sake of it.

Gesture naturally. But just contain your gestures slightly in a television interview. As long as it looks and feels natural, do it.

If you feel self-conscious about gesturing while you speak, try freeing your hands by not clasping them or holding the arms of the chair. This will allow you to tap into your natural ability. Once you start moving your hands, you will be amazed how well you'll capture your audience's attention and convey your meaning.

Voice

Project your natural voice. Diction is important on television and radio. Enunciate the vowel sounds clearly. Break up your sentences, pause and breathe — remember to slow down. Pay attention to pace. (Refer to Chapter 4 for more information about using your voice effectively.)

Clothing

> '*If I want to knock a story off the front page, I just change my hairstyle.*' — Hillary Clinton, former US Secretary of State

How do you want to be perceived? Avoid busy patterns, stripes and spots on television as they can strobe. Think about the message you what to get across and the audience you're presenting to. Obviously a jacket is better for a business audience; classic clothes are best if you're doing something more formal; smart casual or a team uniform may also be part of your message.

Women are always better to wear a two-piece outfit, that is, a top and trousers or a top and skirt; this makes it much easier for the technician to camouflage the microphone cable. Avoid short skirts, low-cut or flimsy tops (they are very difficult to attach microphones to). Other distractions, such as dangly earrings, can be a problem.

Men should avoid wearing ties that clash with their shirts or suit jackets. Pay attention to detail: if you're going to wear a tie, make sure it is properly done up at the neck, sitting straight, and that the collar of your shirt is sitting neatly beneath your jacket. Refer to Chapter 15 on image and grooming for more information.

Stay calm, focus, relax, and have faith in yourself. You are an expert in your field. Tell yourself this. Use positive self-talk and affirmations as discussed in Chapter 11. Warm-up your voice if you are in a quiet place and practise some breathing exercises. This is particularly important before a television interview. Stretch, move around to get your blood pumping and centre yourself by quietly warming or limbering up your body. Anything you do to relax your mind is good. Laughing releases endorphins that will make you feel confident. Yawning opens the back of the throat, which also relaxes the jaw; humming exercises the vocal cords.

Do what is best for you. You more than anyone know what relaxes and energizes you. I often go for a walk a couple of hours before an important interview to run through my messages, then shower and freshen up. I like to be alone so I can stay with the job in-hand.

Media photographs

As the saying goes, 'a photograph is worth a thousand words'. Photographs are the new currency of the media and are highly sought after. Journalists are always after photographs, whether they work in traditional media, online, or even on radio. If you want to engage with the media make sure you can offer them good photos of you, your people, your work environment and the story you're trying to interest them in.

Talk to journalists in advance about what they want, what formats they can work with and the level of resolution they need to reproduce the photo well. If you don't have staff that do this as part of their job, make sure the people who have to do it get training.

Even though a majority of people have smart phones that take photos, tablets and digital cameras, they don't necessarily know how to frame-up a good photo, make it interesting, and make sure it is properly lit. Nor do they know how to group themselves for a 'winning' media shot or even pose for a good head and shoulders photo. This is all part of good presentation, so it's well worth taking practice shots of your team, using any of the devices listed. Review them, or play them back and look at how you can improve them.

Many media photographers are open to running training sessions on all these issues, so two or three hours of their time may be worth its weight in gold. Compelling photos are central to telling your story in the media, on your website, your Facebook page or even in your annual report. My advice is never go past a professional photographer if you can afford one. Also a note of caution: if you want your photos to be used in the media, it's nearly always better to use an experienced media photographer.

Common pitfalls

No comment

Never say 'no comment' in response to a question. You'll look as if you have something to hide. If you can't comment, say so and give a reason why, such as: 'I can't answer that question because the information is confidential' or 'I don't have that information right now, let me get back to you.'

On and off the record

As discussed, nothing is ever 'off the record', so don't put yourself in a vulnerable position by sharing information you don't want the journalist to use; whatever you say can end up in the media in one way or another.

Some good journalists still refuse to allow you to tell them anything 'off the record'. Very simply, it's not in their interest to listen, and it places them in a compromising position if they hear the same information from another source.

With the advent of WikiLeaks and many other major global leaks, revealed almost weekly, leaks are now ubiquitous online and in the mainstream media. Privacy and surveillance are two of the big debates of the 21st century. An increasingly cynical public, which frequently feels disempowered, is always awake to the possibility of revealing the 'dirty tricks' or 'dirty linen' of organizations it doesn't like.

Watch your tongue

Keep your answers brief. Say what you want to say then wait for the next question. Journalists often pause a moment before asking their next question; sometimes interviewees feel uncomfortable with silence and rush to fill the gap with more information than they originally intended to provide. Say what you intend to say and then stop talking.

Be aware of what you say when the interview is 'officially' over. Journalists get some of their best stories in the toilets or in the elevator on the way out.

Jargon

Jargon, beauracratese, gobbledygook and 'weasel words' are the bane of most journalists' lives. Use everyday language, say it simply, and remember to take the audience, who doesn't know what you know, along with you. People who can turn science, technology, engineering or medicine into colourful everyday language are highly sought-after as interview subjects. The very best of them even win awards for their communication skills. In the end it is always about making your subject or issue understandable and interesting to the public.

Listen carefully to the question

Don't let the reporter put words in your mouth. Never repeat inflammatory words fed to you in the question line.

Be prepared to say 'I don't know'

It's all right to tell a journalist you don't know the answer to their question. Always try to suggest someone who might be able to help, or research and get back to them later.

Never lie in an interview. Even a white lie has the ability to land you in hot water; and one small exaggeration or twist on the truth and you instantly lose credibility for everything you say. Likewise, never pass on hearsay or rumour. If you are asked about something that concerns someone else, refer the reporter to that person for comment.

Can I read the story before it goes to print?

Journalists pride themselves on being fair and impartial. Asking if you can preview a story before it goes to print implies that you don't trust them. In simple terms, if it's daily news they don't have time. So, don't embarrass yourself by asking. The journalist will refuse and you'll have antagonized them before they've even written their story.

The two exceptions are usually if the subject matter is technical or if it's a personal feature story.

Other things

- Don't use the host's name all the time. Once at the beginning and once at the end of the conversation is enough. It sounds false if you keep using their name constantly. You're probably not close buddies, and if you are it's probably not a good idea for the public to know about it. Another reason for not constantly dropping the interviewer's name is that stories are frequently made by more than one journalist, so constant reference to one of them can make the story difficult to edit.

- Greetings. If you are being interviewed live and the host greets you, there's no need to ask how they are. For example, if the announcer says, 'We're talking to Professor Stephanie Black from Boston University ... Good morning, Stephanie,' Stephanie should simply say, 'Good morning' and wait for the first question. Asking, 'How are you?' is superfluous and prevents the interviewer from getting on with the job.

- Stay poised and end well — listen for cues for the 'wind-up' and be ready to give a succinct concluding answer. Say thank you, look at the journalist, count to three, hold your composure, and wait for the camera operator to tell you it's over before you react or make inappropriate comments.

'People might not always like what you are saying, but if they think you are authentic as a person they will at least listen — because they will know you are not trying to put one over them.'
— Helen Clark, administrator of the United Nations Development Programme (UNDP)

TIPS ON SUCCESSFUL MEDIA INTERVIEWS

- **Prepare, prepare, prepare.** Key facts, interesting anecdotes, examples and stories should all be on your list.

- **Get clear on the story.** Identify the angle, why you've been asked to comment or the reason the story is suddenly making headlines.

- **Have something to say.** Don't sit on the fence. Be bold, new and fresh.

- **Be warm and professional.** This will always shine through in your interview.

- **Pay attention to what you wear.** Ask yourself how you want to be perceived.

- **Body language matters.** Journalists and viewers will pick up on subtle signals, so ensure your facial expressions and gestures are consistent with your message.

- **Speak clearly and slow down,** especially during broadcast interviews.

- **Get to the point.** An interview is not the time to waffle.

18
Evaluating Your Presentation

'Tell me the truth — I can take it!'

— Maggie Eyre

B eing evaluated by others is never easy. The only way we can improve is to allow others with more experience to review our performance. Put your ego aside. How do you think top presenters became so good at public speaking? Other speakers, teachers and mentors helped them to refine their skills.

Ask for feedback after every time you speak in public. When I pitch for new business I always ask a colleague to have a 'debrief' with me after the presentation. How did I go in that meeting? Did I listen enough? Did I take too long to get to the point? Did I go off on a tangent? Feedback on these points helps me to improve my presentation next time around.

Asking for feedback or planting a friend in the audience to comment on my performance is the best way I know to improve my presentation skills.

Put your ego away

Constructive criticism of your presentation is not criticism of you as a person. Have the confidence and self-belief not to take feedback as a personal attack, but simply as a way of improving your presentation skills.

'The ego is a fascinating monster.'

— Alanis Morissette, singer and performer

During one of my 'Train the Trainer' workshops, I recall a consultant who refused to be evaluated. He was a great presenter, but was afraid of his presentation skills being criticized. Accepting constructive feedback hasn't always been easy for me either; it's tempting to feel I've failed miserably if a presentation hasn't received a glowing evaluation. When I suggest to clients that they might be feeling insecure about feedback, some laugh and say they're fine, but years later they sometimes admit they weren't able to distinguish between feedback on their performance and criticism of themselves as a person. Self-acceptance comes with many years of practice. Remind yourself of that whenever you feel some insecurity coming on.

Feedback is an important part of the learning process. Even if the feedback is offered in a clumsy manner, focus on the learning point instead of taking things personally. And remember, you don't have to agree with every comment. It's only one person's opinion.

Get it in writing

Evaluation forms are excellent because you can refer to them later and refresh your memory about key learning points. If you are receiving verbal feedback, take some notes rather than relying on your memory.

If you are appearing on radio or television get someone to tape it and debrief the outcome with someone you respect. You can usually buy a copy of the interview from the television station. I also do this with print interviews, as it's the only way I learn how I can do better next time. It's not obsessive — it's professional and shows you care about the quality of the work you do.

Watch and read the audience

The audience's reactions are the best indicator of your presentation's success. They will let you know with their body language, their comments and their applause. Stay around afterwards to find out what they think. You will know by the number of people who come up to you. I get some of my best feedback when I allow time to speak to people afterwards.

Don't be afraid to ask, what did you learn? I love it when I receive an email from a stranger telling me what they took away from my speech, or see someone taking notes during a presentation.

If you're in the audience and have been particularly impressed with a presentation, please take the time to let the presenter know, either in person or in writing. I promise they will really appreciate it, regardless of how experienced they are at public speaking. After attending an entertaining and inspiring speech by the award-winning Glenda Jackson, British former actor and politician, I sent her a copy of my written feedback on her presentation, simply because I know how important it is for speakers to know how their audience reacted. She phoned immediately to thank me and commented on how much she appreciated it. We all need feedback.

Before your presentation, always share your speech with someone for critiquing, paying particular attention to the beginning and ending. Likewise, ask someone to cast an eye over any written material you intend to distribute during the presentation — spelling and grammar mistakes make you look sloppy. You may even get some new ideas or anecdotes that you can work into your speech.

Guidelines for giving feedback

Giving feedback is a huge responsibility. You can easily devastate a person's confidence with throwaway comments especially if the person is relatively inexperienced. You have a responsibility to ensure that your comments are well thought through and empowering. Ask yourself, 'If I was receiving this feedback, how would I like to receive it?'

The following suggestions are intended for one-on-one feedback sessions and also group evaluation sessions. They can be useful when writing reports or when giving feedback in person, online or over the phone.

Focus on the positive first

Praise is essential when people have done well. People need to hear what they've done well, in addition to what they can improve on. Follow the Commend — Recommend — Commend sequence of feedback.

For example:

[Commend] 'Your energy is motivating and I love your enthusiasm for your subject.'

[Recommend] 'However, I feel your speech could have less jargon it in and it needs more anecdotes so you connect more with us.'

[Commend] 'Regardless of this you radiated warmth and had great eye contact.'

Be constructive

If you do have observations or comments, make them constructive. This will help the person to find out what they need to do to improve. Giving only positive feedback or just telling them what they are doing wrong is not helpful.

Emphasize what you see and hear

Make your feedback descriptive rather than evaluative. Describe your own observations without making judgments as to whether you see the facts as good or bad, and leave the person to make their own assessment. 'Did you know you said "um" ten times during your introduction?' is better than 'You sounded nervous and ill-prepared.'

Be specific

Make feedback specific rather than general. It is easier for someone to react to this than to general statements. Be straightforward and use objective, not emotional, words. Instead of a broad comment such as 'Your speech was too technical,' be clear about what part of the speech you're referring to, such as 'When you talked about car maintenance, you assumed that your audience knew the different parts of the engine.'

Be realistic

Direct your comments towards actions that the presenter can control. Make your feedback practical and realistic, including specific suggestions for how they can improve. Take into account the experience of the person to whom you're giving feedback — the type of feedback you give an experienced presenter will be different from that for a person who has just given their first public address.

Encourage self-criticism

People are more willing to accept criticism when they recognize their own strengths and weaknesses. Start by encouraging them to appraise themselves and then build on their own insights. I like to ask clients to review their own performance after seeing it on video.

But nothing

Watch out for 'but' when giving positive feedback. Saying, 'You were great, but ...' is a mixed message and can be confusing.

Pick your points

If you overwhelm the person with too many suggestions they are likely to feel frustrated. Focus on the points that need the most improvement.

Focus on them, not you

Feedback is about helping the person receiving the feedback, not demonstrating your superior knowledge. Also, be aware that you can only offer your opinion and the person receiving the feedback doesn't have to agree with you. Using 'I' statements, such as 'I became confused when you jumped between topics' helps the person to realize that you are offering your opinion, and that other people in the audience may feel differently.

When there's a group

If you're debriefing with a team of people, appoint someone to lead the feedback session. This ensures that everyone gets the chance to share their opinion with the group.

Implementing the advice

Receiving feedback can be frustrating if there isn't an opportunity to practise the suggestions in the near future. When receiving feedback, try to set up another speaking engagement with a support buddy so you can put the feedback into practice.

When giving feedback, check that the person has understood what you're saying by asking them to tell you what points they have learned from the feedback session.

Watch for body language

You can often tell how the person is responding to the feedback through their body language. If you sense they are feeling vulnerable or unhappy, limit the feedback to one or two points and focus on building their confidence.

Keep an eye on your own body language as well. If your words are in conflict with your tone or facial expression, the person receiving the feedback will believe your body language rather than the words you say.

Evaluation sheet

Develop your own evaluation sheet based on this suggested outline.

RATING:

5 *Excellent:* very happy with the presentation

4 *Very good:* quite rewarding to listen to

3 *Competent:* some good points, some not so good

2 *Needs work:* somewhat disappointing to listen to

1 *Very disappointing:* take the opportunity to improve and up-skill

*Example. **Opening: Rating 5: Comments:** You started with a powerful personal story which captured our attention immediately.

CATEGORY	RATING	COMMENTS
OPENING Was the opening stimulating and powerful? Did it capture the audience's attention? Did it have impact?	1 2 3 4 5	
MANNER Direct, confident, genuine, calm, professional, lively, bold, powerful, gentle, caring?	1 2 3 4 5	
CONTENT Was there a logical beginning, middle, end? Did the speaker use stories or metaphors to illustrate points? Is the content relevant?	1 2 3 4 5	
BODY LANGUAGE Natural, relaxed gestures, good posture? Confident, expressive?	1 2 3 4 5	

CATEGORY	RATING	COMMENTS
FACIAL EXPRESSION Smiling, expressive, open, no twitching?	1 2 3 4 5	
EYE CONTACT Alive, energetic, looking at the audience?	1 2 3 4 5	
VOCAL QUALITY Varied pitch, pauses, good pace, passionate?	1 2 3 4 5	
VOLUME Easy to hear? Projection?	1 2 3 4 5	
LANGUAGE Is it appropriate for the audience? Jargon?	1 2 3 4 5	
GROUP PARTICIPATION Did the audience get involved? Any questions?	1 2 3 4 5	
TONE Energetic and enthusiastic? Passionate or boring?	1 2 3 4 5	
ENDING Powerful, memorable, challenging, finishes with a bang?	1 2 3 4 5	

STRENGTHS — Three things the speaker did

1. _____

2. _____

3. _____

OPPORTUNITIES — Three things the speaker could improve on

1. _____

2. _____

3. _____

OTHER COMMENTS

_____

Acknowledgements

I would like to thank my publishing team at Exisle: Gareth St John Thomas and Benny Thomas, Anouska Jones, Jody Lee, Mark Robinson and Carole Doesburg. To feel part of the Exisle family is to be part of a home that never stops inspiring, giving and asking me to produce the best work I have in me. Gareth and Benny, you have played a pivotal part in my writing career since 2007. I value your support, feedback and guidance with this revision. It is a privilege to be an author under the well-respected Exisle brand.

Thank you for watching over *Speak Easy* as it goes even further out into the world. It's because of your dedication and belief in me that readers in so many countries now have access to my book.

Special thanks to my most valued assistant Stephanie Clews with whom I have worked in two countries. Throughout the writing of this book you managed my days and provided the necessary calm without which I would never have made my deadline. Thank you for giving me a push and taking over my social media. You are my golden girl.

Allie Webber, thank you for being Fresh Eyre's 'content queen' down under. You bring over 30 years of journalism, wisdom and media knowledge to our programmes. It's because of your contribution to many of the chapters, especially the media chapter, that they are bolder and better. I honour our business and personal friendship and it's also a joy to work alongside you because you bring laughter and play into my life. I appreciate your supervision and plain-speaking honesty as it urges me to go that extra step up in everything I undertake. I'm blessed to know you.

To the unique and talented Lorae Parry, thank you for your filming, editing, voice work and creativity in our workshops. Your comedic skills have our clients in fits of laughter. We have worked internationally for a number of years and I cherish our tight friendship. You bring discipline, compassion and entertainment to our 'Creating Presence' programmes. I can't acknowledge you enough for the long hours of editing and total commitment you give to our clients. Like me, they give you rave reviews!

My dearest journo friend Giulia Sirignani, I have shared the last three revisions of this book with you and each time you speak the truth when reading my work. You are like that unshakeable fan in the stands as you watch me play. You encourage, applaud but also call out the truth when it warrants. I can always count on you to give me the feedback and friendship that is so perfectly balanced and intertwined that I am called to step into the best version of myself. You accept me. You are family. And your Italian home is one that I also call my own. Your health scare in 2015 is another reminder to me that life is precious. I acknowledge you for your courage and the friendship we share.

Jane Eyre, for her superb drawings in the book. Thank you for adding value to the pages and bringing key messages to life by using the stroke of a pencil. I am blessed to have you as my sister-in-law. May this be the beginning of future projects together on other books. You are one of life's treasures.

My talented friend Maggie Warbrick who has always persisted with her vision, which knows no boundaries, of my work. We have had the opportunity to deliver presentation training together in multiple markets throughout Europe, the Middle East and the United Kingdom. Your ideas are always spot on and our relationship blossoms between Stockholm and New Zealand. Thank you for helping me to build my brand and insisting on excellence. We are a dynamic teaching duo!

Linda Cartwright, thank you for your help with the voice chapter and doing exceptional work with my clients for over 20 years. Your technical expertise has made a difference to thousands of people in business and the performing arts. We go way back to my days in the theatre, film and television and still, I'm learning from you. You are a big talent and one of the most generous people I know.

Vivien Sutherland Bridgwater, for giving me ongoing and endless moral support and for generating exciting work with so many clients. You are my biggest advocate in business and have opened up influential doors. Thank you for making a stand for me and persuading business leaders to rehearse with my team. But it's your personal contribution that I honour and thank you most for — your awesome strength and unshakeable faith in me. Thank you for being my confidante, thank you for pushing me back out into the limelight when I wanted to remain private and thank you for the steadfast stream of honesty and integrity. Your belief in me inspires me to produce my best and the winners are my clients because they reap the benefits. I do some of my best writing at your lake house sanctuary while listening to the waterfall in the native, lush bush. You are a legend in my eyes and I thank you for sharing your three children with me and including me in your tight family.

My dear friend, Professor Marilyn Waring, you have always found time to critique my work and listen, I thank you for your understanding, care and unconditional love. I am grateful for everything you have done for me in my personal and professional life. Your work with women all over the world and in the area of human rights moves and inspires me. Thank you for believing in me and standing by me for 37 years. You call on me to improve myself in my work by regularly asking that question that I never thought of. We have been there for each other in our times of grief and joy. I would have it no other way.

I want to thank my extraordinary friend Helen Clark, former prime minister of New Zealand, for endorsing my books from when I began publishing in 2003 and her generous forewords and quotes. It's an honour to be your friend. Your work in the United Nations and your commitment to improving the lives and destinies of so many across the planet has my humble respect. I stand with you in your continued fight for social justice. Your endorsement is not taken for granted.

Alison Gray, your attention to detail and at times brutal honesty served my book. Thank you for asking me the tough questions when you looked at a number of chapters.

Eddie, my eldest brother; thank you for being a positive light in my life especially after our mother's death. I am blessed to have you as a brother, neighbour and co-sharer of life's 'stuff'. You take over tasks to allow me to write and work. And we take care of each other as members of the same committed team and village. My thank you list to you is long and I cherish you just as our mum did.

To my other much-loved brothers Tony, Michael and Robert. I am also forever grateful for your support, love and practical advice. Your continued interest in my writing is always appreciated. Thank you for your unflagging interest in this book. Your children, my nine nieces and nephews, are a credit to you.

Thank you to all my other associates at Fresh Eyre Ltd, including Daniel Greenwood and Margaret Koski. Because of your excellent work, our clients get excellent results.

Lastly and most importantly I honour the memory of my mother. I thank her for giving me the privilege of looking after her in the last two years of her life, right until her last breath at 94 years old. She taught me to be strong and independent and I carry her in my heart through every moment even as I miss terribly her wit, interest, counsel and feedback. I am grateful for all the intimate and open conversations we had about politics, values, career and family. Mum was my biggest fan and my silent support. It was after her death in 2014 that I began writing again, intent on being the teacher and writer she always believed me to be.

I dedicate my life's work to Jean Violet Eyre.

Bibliography

Adler, Stella, *The Technique of Acting*, New York, 1990.

Barkworth, Peter, *About Acting*, London, 1991.

Bell, Chip and Zemke, Ron, *Managing Knock Your Socks Off Service*, New York, 1992.

Bradley, Dinah, *Hyperventilation Syndrome*, Auckland, 2000.

Braysich, Joseph, *Body Language*, New York, 1979.

Brown Glaser, Connie and Steinberg Smalley, Barbara, *More Power to You*, London, 1992.

Buzan, Tony, *Make the Most of Your Mind*, New York, 1988.

Cairnes, Margot, *Approaching the Corporate Heart*, Sydney, 1998.

Callingham, Judy and Edwards, Brian, *How to Survive and Win with the Media*, Auckland, 2000.

Chapman, Elwood, *Your Attitude is Showing*, London, 1992.

Chopra, Deepak, *Ageless Body, Timeless Mind*, Sydney, 1993.

Colbin, Annemarie, *Food and Healing*, New York, 1996.

Decker, Bert, *The Art of Communicating*, California, 1988.

Desikachar, *The Heart of Yoga*, Vermont, 1995.

Dryden, Gordon and Vos, Jeanette, *The Learning Revolution*, Auckland, 1993.

Eswaran, Vijay, *In the Sphere of Silence*, Singapore, 2005.

Evans, Eileen, *It's a Great Life When You're Well*, Auckland, 2000.

Farhi, Donna, *The Breathing Book*, Sydney, 1996.

Fisher, Helge; Knox, Jacqueline; Robinson, Lynne and Thomson, Gordon, *The Official Body Control Pilates Manual*, London, 2000.

Gawain, Shakti, *Creative Visualization*, California, 1978.

Gelb, Michael, *Present Yourself*, California, 1988.

Greene, Bob and Winfrey, Oprah, *Make the Connection*, New York, 1995.

Godefroy, Christian and Barrat, Stephanie, *Confident Public Speaking*, London, 1999.

Henderson, Robyn, *How to Master Networking*, Sydney, 1997.

His Holiness the Dalai Lama, *The Little Book of Wisdom*, London, 1998.

Howard, Ken, *Act Natural*, New York, 2003.

Jampolsky, Gerald, *Love is Letting Go of Fear*, California, 1979.

Lamerton, Jacey, *Everything You Need to Know — Public Speaking*, Glasgow, 2001.

Leigh, Andrew and Maynard, Michael, *Perfect Presentation*, London, 2003.

Linklater, Kristen, *Freeing the Natural Voice*, New York, 1976.

Maltz, Maxwell, *Psycho-cybernetics*, New York, 1987.

Macnamara, Jim and Peart, Joseph, *The New Zealand Public Relations Handbook, 2nd edition*, Palmerston North, 1996.

Maysonave, Sherry, *Casual Power*, Texas, 1999.

Moss, Geoffrey, *Persuasive Presentations*, Wellington, 1994.

Peoples, David, *Presentation Plus*, New York, 1992.

Pante, Robert, *Dressing to Win*, New York, 1984.

Pease, Allan and Barbara, *The Definitive Book of Body Language*, London, 2004.

Ratcliffe, Gail, *Take Control of Your Life*, Sydney, 1995.

Rodenburg, Patsy, *The Right to Speak*, London, 1993.

Stanislavski, Constantin, *An Actor's Handbook*, New York, 1963.

Stuttard, Marie, *The Power of Speech*, Auckland, 1994.

Tourles, Stephanie, *365 Ways to Energize Body and Mind*, Vermont, 2000.

Walters, Lilly, *Secrets of Superstar Speakers*, New York, 2000.

Whiticker, Alan J., *Speeches that Shaped the Modern World*, Sydney, 2005.

Index

function arrangements 176
prepared answers 91–2
for research 80
tough ones 232
quotes, favourite 138

R

Radcliffe, Dr Gail 18, 19
reading aloud 49, 112, 121, 132, 133–4
rehearsal director 126
rehearsals
    business pitches 124–6
    dress rehearsals 122–3
    filming 122
    importance of 117
    number of 118
    opening lines 68
    practice technique 12–13
    purpose of 116
    questions and answers 125–6
    read-throughs 121
    running 127
    in a studio environment 41
    technical 152–3
    using autocue 157
relaxation 22, 27, 113, 191–2
repetition, use of 83
reputation, damage to 221–2
résumés 69–70
rituals 106–7
Roosevelt, Eleanor 4, 6, 144
Roth, Alain 217

S

Schwarzenegger, Arnold 31
screen size, presentations 167–8
seating arrangements 177–9
Seinfeld, Jerry
    on audiences 92
    fear of public speaking 6–7
self-belief 10, 12, 149
self-criticism, encouraged 243
self-promotion 69
self-trust 144
semi-circle/U-shape seating 178
serotonin 19–20
set, dressing it up 67
Shakespeare, William 29, 42, 174
shyness, hiding behind 47
sign language interpreters 123–4
Single Overriding Communication Objective
    (SOCO) 131, 227
Sirignani, Giulia 17
Skype

coaching on 154–6
interviews 163, 165–6
preparing to use 156
tips 173
sleep 23–4
Smith, Dr Gwendolyn 143
social media 15, 157, 173, 221
soundbites 231
speaking visually 230
speech anxiety 46
speech impediment 12
speech quality, voice 57
speeches
    clarity of message 97–8
    commemorative 215
    content 78–9
    context 77–8
    endings 89–90, 131–3
    family celebrations 213
    inappropriate 210–11
    inspirational 215–17
    length of 93–4, 121
    pace of speaking 58
    pauses built in 58–9
    preparation for 11
    recording 122
    structure 81–2
    thank you speeches 213–14
    three-point plan 59
    twenty-first birthday 213
    weddings 209–12, 212
    work farewells/welcomes 214
    writing 75–8, 90, 129
    see also openings; rehearsals
spotlights 177
stage fright 16–18, 129–30
stage lighting 41
statistics
    Facebook 159
    technology usage 150–1
    Twitter 161–2
    using 89
    websites 158
stories, telling 85–6, 230
stress
    effects of 19–22, 140
    four-stage cycle 18–19
    management 183–8
    reducing 20–2, 140–5
stuttering, overcoming 52, 59
style, clothing 200–1
subtext 128–9
summarizing, learning how 231
support team 13–14

Waterford City & County Libraries

WITHDRAWN